Every Knee Shall Bow!
The Case for Christian Universalism

Thomas Allin and Mark T. Chamberlain

xulon
PRESS

Copyright © 2005
by Thomas Allin and Mark T. Chamberlain

Every Knee Shall Bow
by Thomas Allin and Mark T. Chamberlain

Printed in the United States of America

ISBN 1-594679-57-6

All rights reserved solely by the author. The author guarantees all contents are original and do not infringe upon the legal rights of any other person or work. No part of this book may be reproduced in any form without the permission of the author. The views expressed in this book are not necessarily those of the publisher.

Except where noted, Scripture quotations are from the Holy Bible, English Standard Version (ESV), copyright © 2001 by Crossway Bibles, a division of Good News Publishers. Used by permission. All rights reserved.

Scripture taken from the New American Standard Bible (NASB), copyright © 1960, 1962, 1963, 1968, 1971, 1972, 1973, 1975, 1977, 1995 by The Lockman Foundation. Used by permission.

Scripture taken from the Holy Bible, New International Version (NIV), copyright © 1973, 1978, 1984 by the International Bible Society. Used by permission of Zondervan Publishing House. All rights reserved.

Scripture quotations marked (NLT) are taken from the Holy Bible, New Living Translation, copyright © 1996. Used by permission of Tyndale House Publishers, Inc., Wheaton, Illinois 60189. All rights reserved.

Scripture taken from *The Message,* copyright © by Eugene H. Peterson, 1993, 1994, 1995. Used by permission of NavPress Publishing Group.

Scripture taken from *The Emphasized Bible* by Joseph Bryant Rotherham, published in 1994 by Kregel Publications.

www.xulonpress.com

Table of Contents

Introduction vii
Original Preface ix
Chapter 1.   The Question Stated 11
Chapter 2.   The Traditional View Completely Unacceptable 17
Chapter 3.   Why Endless Torment? 37
Chapter 4.   Eternal Hell? Unbelievable! 41
Chapter 5.   We Were All Made for Heaven 45
Chapter 6.   All Shall Live in Christ! 49
Chapter 7.   The Immutability of God 53
Chapter 8.   Universalism in Church History 55
Chapter 9.   Universalism and Creation 63
Chapter 10. What the Old Testament Teaches 65
Chapter 11. What the New Testament Teaches 71
Chapter 12. What the New Testament Teaches, Continued 93
Chapter 13. Objections Answered 107
Chapter 14. What About Evangelism? 113
Chapter 15. Summary and Conclusion 117
Bibliography 123

Introduction

This book started out as a revision of a book written in the nineteenth century by Thomas Allin called *Universalism Asserted*. I don't know much about him except that since a co-worker gave me a copy of his book, he has become a very good friend. I love to read! I have read hundreds of books, most of them theology books. I have read books by Catholics and Protestants, Calvinists and Arminians. My friend's Thomas Allin book is my favorite next to the Bible. I have long suspected the things he wrote about but had never heard them articulated or seen them in print. Then my friend Leone gave me this book, and I KNEW it was true. It is full of Scripture and quotes from the earliest writings of the Church. Anyway, I started out saying that this started out as a revision. It has become something else—a collaboration across the centuries. That is why I list myself as co-author. I don't think my friend Thomas would mind.

Original Preface

Universalism Asserted seems to me to fill a great want of the day; a book was needed which should face fairly and thoroughly the subject of future punishment, for although there are many works on the subject, they either face one aspect of the matter only, or they are written for scholars only, not for the multitude. Mr. Allin's writing is emphatically writing which can be "understood of the people," and surely his book must kill the false accusation so often made that those who believe in the ultimate triumph of Christ, and in the Redemption of the world, make light of sin.

Far from being a weak sentimentalist who shrinks from the thought of suffering, the Universalist, as Mr. Allin shows very conclusively in his second and third chapters, is convinced that every sin meets with its just and remedial punishment; he points out, too, how very injurious is the moral tendency of the popular belief in the everlasting existence of evil, in a purposeless suffering, in an unjust and revolting system of torture. And all this is written calmly and thoughtfully, with a view to meeting the difficulties of those who are in doubt on the subject. Perhaps the most interesting part of the book is that which shows how throughout the entire history of the Church the belief in Universal salvation has been held by many of the best and truest of Christ's followers. And to my mind one of the finest touches is the description given in chapter 1 of the position of those who, shrinking from the current notions of hell and dissatisfied with that most unsatisfying theory—conditional immortality—take refuge in saying that nothing can be definitely known, and that they are content to wait in uncertainty.

The sympathetic way in which the writer meets their position, and his fearless exposure of the dangerous vagueness which lurks beneath its apparent humility, are beyond praise. How is it possible that those who know the depths of sin and ignorance, those who hear the character of God slandered by believers and unbelievers, those who love the ones who pass unrepentant into the Unseen should rest satisfied, while retaining in their hearts even a shadow of a doubt that "As in Adam all die, so in Christ shall all be made alive"?

The old merciless teaching is still taught; there yet remains in many a nursery, as well, alas! as in many a missionary school abroad, a well-known book called *Peep of Day.* In this, little children are allowed to read such doggerel as the following:

> Now if I fight, or scratch, or bite,
> In passion fail, or bad names call,
> Full well I know where I shall go.
> Satan is glad when I am bad,
> And hopes that I with him shall lie,
> In fire and chains, and dreadful pains.
> All liars dwell with him in hell,
> And many more who cursed and swore,
> And all who did what God forbid.

Surely it is time that everyone who believes that the Everlasting Father lovingly, eternally, educates all His children should speak out plainly, and not be ashamed to confess with the Psalmist, "My trust is in the tender mercy of God for ever and ever."

Edna Lyall
Eastbourne
16 December 1890

CHAPTER 1

The Question Stated

Shall not the Judge of all the earth do what is just?
(Genesis 18:25)

Both the original author and the reviser of this work are Evangelical Christians. We believe that the Bible is the inspired, infallible Word of God. The only major difference in our beliefs and those of other Evangelicals is that when the Bible makes statements such as that in 1 John 4:14, "The Father has sent his Son to be the Savior of the world," we believe they are literally true. That is, we believe that if the Father sent the Son to save the world, the world is going to be saved! To me, any other view basically means that the Son of God was unable to accomplish what the Father sent Him to do!

The popular belief that many will end up in a place of torment forever without the possibility of ever being forgiven is considered to be the biblical view, I believe, solely on the basis of misinterpretations of biblical imagery, by mistranslations and misconceptions of the true meaning of the original text, and finally, by completely ignoring the vast body of evidence in favor of the ultimate salvation of all men. This will be shown by very many passages of the New Testament, no less than by the great principles that pervade the teachings of all of God's revelation to us.

The popular view, as will be shown, was not generally held by the majority of Christians until over four hundred years after the founding of the Church, when it was popularized by Augustine. It is distinctly opposed to the views of many of the holiest and wisest fathers of the church in primitive times, who in so teaching expressed the beliefs of very many, if not the majority, of those of their day. Even Augustine, A.D. 354–430, himself a proponent of eternal torment, had to admit that in his days, "There are very many who, though not denying the Holy Scriptures, do not believe in endless torments."

I once shared some of these facts with someone who replied by saying something like, "I don't care what the early Christians believed. I only care what the Bible says." Would it not have been more accurate to say, "I don't care how the earliest Christians interpreted the Bible—only how I do," or "only how my church does." As if any church is infallible! This kind of ignorant thinking keeps people from even being willing to examine a view that teaches that God is truly a God of kindness, compassion, and forgiveness for everyone, and not a cruel sadist who created millions, perhaps billions, knowing that, whether through their own choice or not, they were destined for a torture chamber infinitely worse than anything the Marquis De Sade, Hitler, or Saddam Hussein could ever dream up because it is infinitely longer in duration!

I believe that for many, many people, the idea that a loving God could cast millions of His creatures into a place of never-ending torment is a huge obstacle to their ever becoming Christians in this life. If He truly wants all men to be saved, it doesn't seem as if He would put such obstacles in people's way. I have had people ask me, "If God is so loving, how can He send millions of people to eternal hell, many of whom have never even heard of Him?" Many Christians will say that they are just making excuses. But try to put aside your preconceived ideas for just a moment and ask yourself, What kind of parent would treat his children this way? "But," you may say, "God's ways are not our ways." No, thank God, they are not. But they are higher, not lower! Would God command us to love our enemies and to forgive our enemies when according to the traditional view, He does not forgive His?

Whenever I tell people that I don't believe a loving God would allow His children to end up in eternal hell, they always answer, "Yes, God is a God of love. But He is also a God of justice." I firmly believe in God's justice, but by what stretch of the imagination can eternal hell be considered just? Especially when it is not only for murderers, rapists, child molesters, and torturers, but also for moral people, religious people, even kind and loving people whose "only" crime is that they didn't pray the sinner's prayer!

Don't get me wrong. I believe in Romans 3:23 that "All have sinned and fall short of the glory of God." I believe that all of us deserve to be punished, but eternal torment?!! Can you honestly look at your unsaved relatives and say that they deserve to be tormented by demons forever? Some would say that teaching the ultimate salvation of all would either weaken or completely remove any belief in future punishment. The exact opposite is true. Most people will only believe us when we say that a just and loving God must punish sin when we teach a plan of punishment that is reasonable and credible. A penalty that seems unspeakably cruel, shocking, even monstrous loses all force as a threat! Only Universalists fully recognize both the guilt of sin and the need for a just punishment, one that fits the crime!

Let me remind you what the traditional view really is: that those who die without being born again by faith in Jesus will be cast into hell where there is endless evil and endless torment! Also, there is no hope for forgiveness, no possibility of reprieve, and no possibility of alleviation of evil, no possibility that a loving God will have pity on His children! After ages and ages of unspeakable agony, their cup of suffering will not be diminished by one single drop, their pain then will be no closer to ending than before!

Those who believe that this terrible doctrine is a part of the "good news of great joy for everyone" differ in their belief as to how many will face this horrible fate. Some believe it will be the majority of mankind, and some a small minority. This difference illustrates the constant revolt of the human heart and conscience against such a cruel doctrine! It seems perfectly clear that the traditional view forces us to believe that the vast majority of mankind will suffer this cruel fate, because according to this view, only those who are truly converted in this life will reach heaven. It is also clear that of all professing Christians, only a few of them are truly converted, to say nothing of the millions who die in paganism, many of them completely ignorant of Jesus Christ! But aside from that, it isn't really about how many will be lost and how many will be saved. The real problem with the traditional view is the infliction of such a cruel penalty at all, not in how many are doomed to it.

Listen to these warnings about hell written by a couple of proponents of the traditional view. If you truly believe these, you should weep from morning till night for anyone who will go to such a place!

> Little child, if you go to hell, there will be a devil at your side to strike you. He will go on striking you every minute forever and ever without ever stopping. The first stroke will make your body as bad as the body of Job, covered, from head to foot, with sores and ulcers. The second stroke will make your body twice as bad as the body of Job. The third stroke will make your body four times as bad as the body of Job. How, then, will your body be after the devil has been striking it every moment for a hundred million of years without stopping? Perhaps, at this moment, seven o'clock in the evening, a child is just going into hell. Tomorrow evening, at seven o'clock, go and knock at the gates of hell and ask what the child is doing. The devils will go and look. They will come back again and say the child is burning. Go in a week and ask what the child is doing; you will get the same answer—it is burning. Go in a year and ask, the same answer comes—it is burning. Go in a million years and ask the same question, and the answer is just the same—it is burning. So if you go forever and ever, you will always get the same answer—it is burning in the fire. (Rev. J. Furniss, *The Sight of Hell*)

Listen to Charles H. Spurgeon, the famous Baptist preacher, if you can stand to after that last charming essay!

> When thou diest, thy soul will be tormented alone, that will be a hell for it: but at the day of judgment thy body will join thy soul, and then thou wilt have twin hells, thy soul sweating drops of blood, and thy body suffused with agony. In fire, exactly like that we have on earth, thy body will lie, asbestos like, forever unconsumed, all thy veins roads for the feet of pain to travel on, every nerve a string, on which the devil shall forever play his diabolical tune of hell's unutterable lament.

If Christians really believe that horrible scenario, they should be wearing themselves out day and night with tears pouring from their eyes, trying to prevent even one precious soul from such a fate! And that horrible place is supposed to be allowed to exist by a loving God? Nonsense! As awful as these quotes are, and many more could be quoted, none of them could even begin to give an adequate idea of the horrors of hell as believed in by Evangelicals, because the most terrifying thing about it—its unendingness—is beyond our power to conceive! Someone might say, "No one believes in a material hell anymore. We no longer teach a literal lake of fire." Praise God! That's an improvement. I would rather "just" be absent from God forever than to be absent from God and be on fire forever too! But that still doesn't change the fact that in your view, sin and suffering are still endless. If evil in any form is allowed to exist forever, the main problem with the traditional view still remains.

CHAPTER 2

The Traditional View Completely Unacceptable

But you, O Lord, are a God merciful and gracious.
(Psalm 86:15)

Let me start out right here with a protest against the totally false view that Christian Universalists have lax views of sin or doctrine. No view so effectively proves God's hatred of sin as this view that teaches that He cannot and will not tolerate its existence forever!

2 Peter 3:13 says, "But according to his promise we are waiting for new heavens and a new earth in which righteousness dwells." The clear implication of this passage is that in the new heavens and new earth, there will only be righteousness, not an everlasting hell filled with unrighteousness!

Next I would like to say that any teaching that says even one soul will be eternally lost strikes a blow at both the incarnation and the atonement! Romans and 1 Corinthians both teach that mankind as a whole has had two representatives, two Adams. The first one through his disobedience brought sin and death on the entire race. The second one, which is Christ, brought salvation for the entire race. 1 Corinthians 15:22: "For as in Adam ALL die, so also in Christ shall ALL be made alive." Romans 5:18 states this same truth: "Therefore, as one trespass led to condemnation for ALL men, so one act of righteousness leads to justification and life for ALL men."

The traditional view of the atonement that it is effective only for the few who receive Christ in this life dishonors the cross by virtually teaching that it was a stupendous failure! This is easy to prove. If any action does not produce the desired results, it is a failure. If I go to a shooting range or an arcade where I'll be shooting a gun, I'm going to aim for the bull's-eye! If I don't even come close, I have failed. Scripture says in 1 John 4:14, as well as many other places, that "The Father has sent his Son to be the Savior of the world!" If God's aim in sending His Son was to save the world and only a pitifully small number of the world are in fact saved, God's aim was not met and the cross is a failure! This conclusion is inescapable, unless of course you don't believe in God's love for the whole world and His desire to save it anyway! In such a case, you don't believe the clear statements of Scripture, because God's desire to save all men is taught explicitly throughout the Bible, especially the New Testament.

Next, I would like to appeal to your conscience. To reconcile the belief in endless evil and misery with the most elementary ideas of justice, fairness, and goodness (not to mention mercy) is completely impossible! Thus, this belief destroys the only basis on which to have any beliefs at all—it sets aside the most basic convictions of our consciences and paralyzes our capability of judging what is right and what is wrong.

In his excellent book, *Mere Christianity*, C.S. Lewis makes a very strong case that God has placed within each one of us an instinctive knowledge of right and wrong. He writes,

> Every one has heard people quarrelling. Sometimes it sounds funny and sometimes it sounds merely unpleasant; but however it sounds, I believe we can learn something very important from listening to the kinds of things they say. They say things like this: "How'd you like it if anyone did the same to you?" "That's my seat, I was there first." "Leave

him alone, he isn't doing you any harm." "Why should you shove in first?" "Give me a bit of your orange, I gave you a bit of mine." "Come on, you promised." People say things like that every day, educated people as well as uneducated, and children as well as grown-ups. Now what interests me about all these remarks is that the man who makes them is not merely saying that the other man's behavior does not happen to please him. He is appealing to some kind of standard of behavior which he expects the other man to know about. And the other man very seldom replies: "To hell with your standard." Nearly always he tries to make out that what he has been doing does not really go against the standard, or that if it does there is some special reason in this particular case why the person who took the seat first should not keep it, or that things were quite different when he was given the bit of orange, or that something has turned up which lets him off keeping his promise. It looks, in fact, very much as if both parties had in mind some kind of Law or Rule of fair play or decent behavior or morality or whatever you like to call it, about which they really agreed.

God has given us the ability to know right from wrong, good from bad, kind from cruel, and He operates by those same standards. If human reason isn't competent to decide for sure whether certain acts said to come from God are evil and cruel, then it is equally incompetent to decide whether other acts of His are just and merciful. What I mean is, if I can't base my beliefs about whether God is good, kind, just, and compassionate on my inner sense of right and wrong, then what can I base them on? If you say, "Base them on God's Word," I'll reply, "If the God set forth in the Bible is not good, kind, just, and compassionate, as He has given me the ability to understand those terms, I refuse to worship Him, and so should you!" But fortunately He is! Psalm 86:15: "But you, O Lord, are a God merciful and gracious!" 1 John 4:8: "God is love!"

Lamentations 3:31–33: "For the Lord will not cast off forever, but, though he cause grief, he will have compassion according to the abundance of his steadfast love; for he does not willingly afflict or grieve the children of men."

Why do I say all this? Simply to say that it should be obvious that the God of everlasting hell is not the kind, loving, just, and compassionate God of the Bible, but a cruel, sadistic monster! And I need not be afraid to say so because God is the one who has given me the ability to think, reason, and judge between what is right and wrong, kind and cruel. God invites us to use our reason in Isaiah 1:18: "Come now, let us reason together, says the Lord: though your sins are like scarlet, they shall be as white as snow; though they are red like crimson, they shall become like wool."

You may quote Romans 9:20 to me: "But who are you, O man, to answer back to God?" Far be it from me to judge or answer back to the true God! I am judging what I believe to be a blasphemous misrepresentation of the true God. I love God! I gladly give Him all glory, honor, and praise because He is perfect, and He is worthy!

But, the idea that we should worship God whether He is good or not, just because He is Almighty (which is really what many Christians believe), is ridiculous! If He is all powerful but not loving, He is to be feared and held in awe, but loved? How can you love someone who is just waiting to cast you into a place of unspeakable agony?

Just think how this doctrine of endless evil and torment must strike a sincere seeker after God. You tell him that God is not only Almighty, but also good, loving, compassionate, and kind. You tell him God is his Father. If he knows anything about this doctrine of eternal torment, he may well say, "You tell me that God is good, that He is a loving Father; but He creates millions of hapless creatures knowing that there is an unspeakably horrible doom waiting for them. He creates these creatures through no will of their own, with a sinful nature that makes them incapable of doing His will, knowing that they are going to spend all eternity apart from Him suffering unspeakable agony, and He not only knows this but also allows it to happen? And you tell me He loves them?! If endless misery is the certain result, known beforehand by God, of bringing me into existence, to force the 'gift' of life on me is the worst thing He could possibly do to me!"

Some think that to believe in the ultimate salvation of all implies the escape of the wicked from all punishment and places the sinner on the same level as the saint. Let me reply once and for all that nothing could be farther from the truth. For the Christian Universalist or the believer in the wider hope, as it has been called, we believe that the very method God uses to bring those who die unsaved into a saving relationship with Christ is the severity of the divine judgment, the consuming fire, that burns up all iniquity. The wider hope teaches the certainty of punishment for the obstinate sinner, because it sees God's judgment as the mode of cure. Unrepented sin leads to an awful future penalty, a penalty that is in proportion to the guilt of the sinner, and is continued until he repents. Christian Universalists not only accept but also emphasize the terrible warning of punishment to come, because they see punishment not as needless cruelty with no purpose, but as both justice and discipline that brings the sinner to repentance.

The main question of the debate is this: Can evil ever be stronger than God? Can a Father allow the endless, hopeless sin and misery of even one of His children, and calmly look on forever and ever, unmoved and unsympathizing? The Bible speaks in Acts 3:21 of a "time for restoring all things" and in 1 Corinthians 15:28 of a time when "God will be ALL IN ALL." And in Colossians 1:20, it speaks of God reconciling ALL things to Himself through Christ! If these verses don't teach the salvation of all, words have no meaning!

People always tell me that all chances for salvation end at a person's death. But where is this taught? The only passage of scripture I have ever read or heard anyone try to use to prove this is Hebrews 9:27. Let's look at it: "And just as it is appointed for man to die once, and after that comes judgment." How does this verse teach that there are no further chances for salvation after death? Where does it say in this verse that after the judgment comes eternal hell? Nowhere! If God wants to hand down a different sentence to each individual according to the light he or she had and the sins that have been committed, why can't He? Jesus taught a parable in Luke chapter 12 that appears to teach that very thing. Luke 12:42–48:

And the Lord said, "Who then is the faithful and wise manager, whom his master will set over his household, to give them their portion of food at the proper time? Blessed is that servant whom his master will find so doing when he comes. Truly, I say to you, he will set him over all his possessions. But if that servant says to himself, 'My master is delayed in coming,' and begins to beat the male and female servants, and to eat and drink and get drunk, the master of that servant will come on a day when he does not expect him and at an hour he does not know, and will cut him in pieces and put him with the unfaithful. And that servant who knew his master's will but did not get ready or act according to his will, will receive a severe beating. But the one who did not know, and did what deserved a beating, will receive a light beating. Everyone to whom much was given, of him much will be required, and from him to whom they entrusted much, they will demand the more."

This parable clearly teaches that there are degrees of punishment after death. The only way this can be true is if the different punishments are different lengths of time. If hell is separation from God and from all good, and it is eternal, then that nice person who lives next door, or your mother or father, or brother or sister, or son or daughter who doesn't know Jesus will suffer as much as Adolph Hitler because the worst possible punishment anyone could endure is separation from God!

The parables of the lost sheep and the lost coin, both taught by Jesus at the same time as the parable of the prodigal son, can be understood to mean that God never gives up on anyone until they come into a saving relationship with His Son Jesus. Luke 15:3–10:

So he told them this parable: "What man of you, having a hundred sheep, if he has lost one of them, does not leave the ninety-nine in the open country, and go after the one that is lost, UNTIL HE FINDS

IT? And when he has found it, he lays it on his shoulders, rejoicing. And when he comes home, he calls together his friends and his neighbors, saying to them, 'Rejoice with me, for I have found my sheep that was lost.' Just so, I tell you, there will be more joy in heaven over one sinner who repents than over ninety-nine righteous persons who need no repentance.

"Or what woman, having ten silver coins, if she loses one coin, does not light a lamp and sweep the house and seek diligently UNTIL SHE FINDS IT? And when she has found it, she calls together her friends and neighbors, saying, 'Rejoice with me, for I have found the coin that I had lost.' Just so, I tell you, there is joy before the angels of God over one sinner who repents."

Don't you see it?! By telling these parables, Jesus was saying, "That's how My Father is! That's how I am! As long as there is one of My Father's children, My brothers and sisters, who is lost, we are going to keep on looking for him UNTIL WE FIND HIM!" Does that sound as if He is going to give up on anybody just because he dies? No!! Look at the story of the prodigal. It should be called "The Story of the Father Who Never Gives Up on His Children!" Luke 15:11–32:

And he said, "There was a man who had two sons. And the younger of them said to his father, 'Father, give me the share of property that is coming to me.' And he divided his property between them. Not many days later, the younger son gathered all he had and took a journey into a far country, and there he squandered his property in reckless living. And when he had spent everything, a severe famine arose in that country, and he began to be in need. So he went and hired himself out to one of the citizens of that country, who sent him into his fields to feed pigs. And he was longing to be fed with the pods that the pigs ate, and no one gave him anything.

"But when he came to himself, he said, 'How many of my father's hired servants have more than enough bread, but I perish here with hunger! I will arise and go to my father, and I will say to him, "Father, I have sinned against heaven and before you. I am no longer worthy to be called your son. Treat me as one of your hired servants."' And he arose and came to his father. But while he was still a long way off, his father saw him and felt compassion, and ran and embraced him and kissed him. And the son said to him, 'Father, I have sinned against heaven and before you. I am no longer worthy to be called your son.' But the father said to his servants, 'Bring quickly the best robe, and put it on him, and put a ring on his hand, and shoes on his feet. And bring the fattened calf and kill it, and let us eat and celebrate. For this my son was dead, and is alive again; he was lost, and is found.' And they began to celebrate."

Suppose that the father had set an arbitrary time limit on when he would forgive his lost son. Suppose he said to himself, "If he comes back within a year, I'll forgive him and take him back. But after that, I'm going to punish him as severely as I possibly can!" Two years later, the boy comes back. What does the father do? If he is a man of his word, he has him tortured and sends him away forever, into the outer darkness where there is weeping and wailing and gnashing of teeth. And as the son is leaving, the father yells after him, "And don't come back! Ever!" This seems to me to be exactly how God would be if He set death as an arbitrary time limit on when people can be saved! But I believe that according to this parable, God our loving Father will be watching and waiting for every one of his lost children, even after earthly death, until every last one is saved!

One argument against Universalism is that it is dangerous.

"The church has to teach eternal hell to restrain sin and scare people into repenting so they can escape the fires of hell." Those who would argue like this don't think about how badly this reflects on God by saying:

(a) He permits His children, made in His image, to sink so low into evil that the only option left to Him in dealing with their sin is punishing them forever;
(b) Knowing this, He either hides, or allows to be hidden, from the vast majority of mankind the only remedy for this situation, which is Jesus; and
(c) He did not say a single word that even hints at eternal punishment in the Old Testament.

Let's look at this argument that eternal hell is a deterrent against sin. If so, why is it that the vast majority of those who hear about it don't get saved? What has the doctrine of eternal hell really accomplished? Has it checked the spread of every kind of sin and immorality from our cities? Can a single sin be named that this teaching has wiped out anywhere? It is no wonder! Most churches preach a God who really loves only those who repent and surely must hate those who don't if He is willing to allow them to suffer unspeakable agony forever! True Christian Universalism, if understood, believed, and proclaimed, would deter from sin because it teaches a just and fair punishment for sin that is meant for correction and that even His punishment springs from love and mercy, not from a sadistic desire to inflict pain forever with out any positive outcome.

Psalm 62:12 says, "To you, O Lord, belongs steadfast love. For you will render to a man according to his work." How can rendering to a man according to his work be an expression of God's love if it results in eternal torment? If that is love, I would rather have hate!

I have heard many people say such things as, "God doesn't send people to hell. They choose it." Oh? Would anyone choose to go to a place of torture forever if he really believed in it? Maybe it is just too incredible for anyone to really believe it! Also, I would like to ask, Why is there so much emphasis on man's free will as if it, instead of God, were the most powerful force in the universe?

Look at the story of the conversion of Saul, the Christian hater, into Paul the Apostle of Jesus Christ found in Acts 9:1–19, and tell me that God can't save all the people He wants, without violating their will or turning them into robots, no matter how unwilling they are!

When we first meet Paul, his name is Saul. He was a witness at the stoning of Stephen, and he gave his hearty consent to the evil deed. In Acts 7:58, 8:1, and 8:3 we read: "And the witnesses laid down their garments at the feet of a young man named Saul. And Saul approved of his execution. ... Saul was ravaging the church, and entering house after house, he dragged off men and women and committed them to prison." But right when "Saul" was "breathing threats and murder against the disciples of the Lord" and trying to wipe out the church, Acts 9:3–6 tells us, "Suddenly a light from heaven flashed around him. And falling to the ground he heard a voice saying to him, 'Saul, Saul, why are you persecuting me?' And he said, 'Who are you, Lord?' And he said, 'I am Jesus, whom you are persecuting. But rise and enter the city, and you will be told what you are to do.'" Saul of course became a believer, and the rest, as they say, is history.

Sundar Singh was a Sikh. His mother brought him up to be a devout Sikh and to have reverence for all religions as she herself did. She took him to see an Indian holy man or Sadhu who saw in him, as she did, the makings of a Sadhu. Sundar did respect other religions as his mother had taught him except the Christian religion and its founder, Jesus. Because of Jesus' exclusive claims, Sundar hated Jesus and anyone who represented Him. He even threw stones at Christians and tore up and burned a Bible. In short, he was not seeking Jesus. But Jesus was seeking him! His mother died when he was a boy. He was filled with anger at the Christians who would have said she was lost because she was not a Christian, and his burning of the Bible gave him a guilty conscience. He had no peace. I'll let him continue his story in his own words:

> Though at the time I had considered myself a hero for burning the Gospel, my heart had no peace. Indeed, my unrest only increased, and I was miser-

able for the next two days. On the third day, when I could bear it no longer, I rose at 3:00 A.M. and prayed that if there was a God at all, he would reveal himself to me. Should I receive no answer by morning, I would place my head on the railroad tracks and seek the answer to my questions beyond the edge of this life. I prayed and prayed, waiting for the time to take my last walk. At about 4:30 I saw something strange. There was a glow in the room. At first I thought there was a fire in the house, but looking through the door and windows, I could see no cause for the light. Then the thought came to me: perhaps this was an answer from God. So I returned to my accustomed place and prayed, looking into the strange light. Then I saw a figure in the light, strange but somehow familiar at once. It was neither Siva nor Krishna nor any of the other Hindu incarnations I had expected. Then I heard a voice speaking to me in Urdu: "Sundar, how long will you mock me? I have come to save you because you have prayed to find the way of truth. Why then don't you accept it?" It was then that I saw the marks of blood on his hands and feet and knew that it was Yesu, the one proclaimed by the Christians. In amazement I fell at his feet. I was filled with deep sorrow and remorse for my insults and my irreverence, but also with a wonderful peace. This was the joy I had been seeking. This was heaven. ... Then the vision was gone, though my peace and joy remained.

C.S. Lewis tells of his conversion in his book *Surprised by Joy*:

You must picture me alone in that room at Magdalen, night after night, feeling, whenever my mind lifted even for a second from my work, the steady, unrelenting approach of Him whom I so earnestly desired not to meet. That which I greatly feared had at last come upon me. In the Trinity term of 1929 I gave in, and admitted that God was God, and knelt and prayed: perhaps that night, the most dejected and reluctant convert in all England. I did not then see what is now the most shining and obvious thing: the divine humility which will accept a convert on such terms. The Prodigal Son at least walked home on his own feet. But who can truly adore that love which will open the high gates to a prodigal who is brought in kicking, struggling, resentful, and darting his eyes in every direction for a chance of escape?

These are just a few of many stories that could be quoted to illustrate the sovereignty of God in salvation. Were they robots after their conversions? Was their love for Jesus any less genuine because He sought them out and revealed Himself to them so unmistakably? Of course not! If God is not able to make anyone willing to be saved, why do we pray for people's salvation? We pray for people to be saved because we know instinctively that God is able to overcome any resistance and save anyone! We pray because we know that God delights in saving people in answer to our prayers! I don't know why some people are saved in this life and others are not, but I am convinced that God is willing and able to save everyone, and that He eventually will! That is why I believe that death does not have the last word.

The idea that we have a totally free will is easily shown to be untrue. Man's choice is limited in many ways. First, we are born with a nature that is prone to sin. Theologians call this tendency "original sin," and if you don't believe in it, just look around you at all the crime, hatred, and cruelty all over the world. Just look honestly into your own heart! Next, look at the facts of life. We have no choice at all as to when or where we were born, factors that are very important in determining what we believe. People who are born in a "Christian" country and raised by Christian parents seem to have a distinct advantage over those who are born in a Muslim, Hindu, Buddhist, or any other kind of culture. People tend to believe whatever they are raised to believe. This hardly seems fair if this brief life is our only opportunity for getting right with God! What the facts point to is that God has granted us a limited freedom to train us, His children, for the enjoyment of perfect freedom in heaven.

Hebrews 12:5–6,11 says, "My son, do not regard lightly the discipline of the Lord, nor be weary when reproved by him. For the Lord disciplines the one he loves, and chastises every son he receives. For the moment all discipline seems painful rather than pleasant, but later it yields the peaceful fruit of righteousness to those who have been trained by it." Couldn't it just be possible that these verses apply not only to Christians, but also to non-Christians of whom Paul says in Acts 17:28: "For we are indeed his offspring"?

Isn't it possible that they apply even to those in hell, and that He sends them there for discipline, chastisement, and training that will later yield the peaceful fruit of righteousness? I hope so! Don't you?

The idea that God will allow his children to suffer everlasting torment in hell to preserve their free will is absurd. I would far rather have a limited freedom that results in eternal salvation than a completely unrestrained freedom that leads to everlasting torment! To argue that because of man's free will he can go on forever rejecting God and choosing evil is really to argue not for human freedom, but for human slavery! What this view is really saying is that to preserve people's dignity, they must be free to become the slaves of evil and the victims of Satan forever! What kind of freedom is that? What would you think of an earthly father who used that kind of reasoning? What if you heard a father say, "I have to allow my son to become a drunk or a drug addict to preserve his sobriety," or if he said, "I have to allow my daughter to be a prostitute to preserve her purity"? No! Someday, every knee will freely bow and every tongue will gladly confess that Jesus Christ is Lord to the glory of God the Father because goodness and love are the strongest forces in a universe ruled by God. To plead against God's sovereignty in saving whoever He will, whenever He will, by saying that it annuls human freedom is as unreasonable as a parent of a sick child objecting to the restraint of the hospital room and the doctors and nurses because the child wants to go home. Sometimes sick children need to be restrained, criminals need to be imprisoned, and sinners need to be drawn to God whether they like it or not, just as Jesus said He would do in John 12:32: "And I, when I am lifted up from the earth, will draw all people to myself."

Let me give you the Calvinist and Arminian translations of this verse. Calvinist: "And I, when I am lifted up from the earth, will draw the elect to myself." Arminian: "And I, when I am lifted up from the earth, will try to draw all people to myself." I guarantee that you can check with any commentary or any Greek scholar, and you will find that neither the Calvinist translation nor the Arminian translation are faithful renderings of the Greek.

If God allows men the freedom to reject Him forever, even though that freedom leads to eternal torment, that would mean that He cares more about their freedom than their salvation! Does that make sense? Of course not. And it is not scriptural either. In Isaiah 46:10, God says, "My counsel shall stand, and I will accomplish all my purpose." Psalm 135:6: "Whatever the Lord pleases, he does, in heaven and on earth, in the seas and all deeps." Proverbs 19:21: "Many are the plans in the mind of a man, but it is the purpose of the Lord that will stand." Proverbs 21:1: "The king's heart is a stream of water in the hand of the Lord; he turns it wherever he will." Ephesians 1:11 says that God "works all things according to the counsel of his will."

How could words possibly be any clearer? God says, "I will accomplish ALL my purpose." It is clearly God's will to save all men according to the following scriptures:

> 1 Timothy 2:3–6: "This is good, and it is pleasing in the sight of God our Savior, who desires all people to be saved and to come to the knowledge of the truth. For there is one God, and there is one mediator between God and men, the man Christ Jesus, who gave himself as a ransom for all, which is the testimony given at the proper time."

> 1 Timothy 4:10: "For to this end we toil and strive, because we have our hope set on the living God, who is the Savior of all people, especially of

those who believe."

John 12:32: "And I [Jesus], when I am lifted up from the earth, will draw all people to myself."

2 Peter 3:9 says that the Lord is "not wishing that any should perish, but that all should reach repentance."

If God does whatever He pleases, and He desires all men to be saved, what can stop Him from saving all men? Is man's will stronger than God? One of the strongest examples in Scripture of free will is Matthew 23:37: "O Jerusalem, Jerusalem, the city that kills the prophets and stones those who are sent to it! How often would I have gathered your children together as a hen gathers her brood under her wings, and you would not!" But a little farther down in verse 39, He says of those who would not that they would one day say, "Blessed is he who comes in the name of the Lord." Let me give an illustration of what kind of a father God would be if He allowed even one of His children to suffer everlasting torment in hell.

Imagine a frail and narrow bridge swinging over the Grand Canyon. On this bridge, rocking back and forth in the wind, a father places his young child. On the other side, the father has placed a prize of inestimable worth, which he promises to give the child if he makes it across the bridge, and then he orders him to cross, commanding him not to look to the left or to the right. The boy, heedless and disobedient, looks around and becomes frightened and slips and falls into the canyon, becoming impaled on a sharp rock below. There he hangs for long agonizing years, writhing in torture, crying out to his father to help him. But his father turns a deaf ear to all his desperate pleas, totally indifferent to the horrible sufferings of his child. He justifies his cruel, sadistic behavior by saying, "I told him how to get across the bridge safely and he didn't listen. It's his own fault he is suffering." Granted our Lord has promised to be with those of us who are His followers, but the rest have no such promise.

Even admitting that he could have made it safely across if he had listened to his father, anyone with an ounce of compassion would have to admit that this father was an evil monster, a sadistic fiend, not a loving father, and yet this is exactly what the false god of tradition does! He places his children on the frail and narrow bridge of life, stretched over the awful, flaming abyss of eternal damnation, with the possibility of heaven beyond. Then he leaves them there to cross it, swinging fearfully in the winds of temptation, knowing that most of them will in crossing be thrown into the horrible pit, to lie there forever in hopeless agony! And this is a God of love?

Well has the poet spoken of such a god:

> And can you then look down from perfect bliss
> And see me plunge into the dark abyss,
> Calling you Father in a sea of fire,
> Or pouring out blasphemies at your desire?

Would a loving Father really do this? In Jonah 4:11, God says to Jonah, "And should I not pity Nineveh, that great city, in which there are more than 120,000 persons who do not know their right hand from their left?" Doesn't God's description of the Ninevites describe all natural men? If in our natural state we don't even know our right hand from our left, would it really be loving or even just to sentence any of us to everlasting torment? This is the question, and no argument can evade it: "Is God good, loving, and just, as He himself has taught us in our consciences and in His Word to understand these terms, or isn't He?" If He isn't, we may as well not worship anything!

But, of course the true God is good—Psalm 34:8: "Oh, taste and see that the Lord is good!" He is love—1 John 4:8: "God is love." And He is just—Deuteronomy 32:4: "The Rock, his work is perfect, for all his ways are justice. A God of faithfulness and without iniquity, just and upright is he."

Amen! Praise His wonderful, matchless name!!!!!

The doctrine of everlasting hell has inspired many professing Christians to commit unspeakable atrocities! They reasoned that if God could light up the gloomy fires of hell and keep them blazing for all eternity, it was an easy, natural step to take to set up in His name a little copy of His justice in anticipation of His sentence!

Queen Mary, also known as Bloody Mary, who persecuted Protestants, said, "As the souls of heretics are hereafter to be eternally burning in hell, there can be nothing more proper than for me to imitate the divine vengeance, by burning them here on earth." Others, both Protestant and Catholic, have persecuted those they considered heretics not only to take vengeance on them, but also in many cases to try to force them to repent so that they might escape the flames of hell.

Thomas Allin writes, "Many pages might be filled in enumerating the horrors, and anguish, added to human life by these doctrines. Let me only add that they have poisoned the very fount of pity and love by representing Him, Whose we are, and before Whom we bow, as calmly looking on during the endless cycles of eternity, at the sin and agony of myriads upon myriads of His creatures."

I have had people tell me, "Heaven and hell are both said to be 'eternal' in Scripture. You can't have one without the other." To paraphrase Thomas Allin, "They would purchase eternal joy in heaven at the terrible cost of the eternal, hopeless torture of the lost." As to the word "eternal," or *aion* or *aionios* as it is in Greek, I will show later that this word by no means needs to be translated as "eternal" but means rather "an age" or "an indefinite period of time." How long of a time depends on the subject.

And as to the idea that Christians can live in eternal bliss while their loved ones are in eternal misery, all I can say is "God deliver me from ever being that cruel and callous!" Let's suppose that the saints in heaven have no memory of the past. Many assume that the story of the rich man and Lazarus found in Luke 16:19–31 is a true story rather than a parable. In this story, Lazarus and the rich man could see each other and communicate with one another. If I were in heaven, or paradise, or wherever, and I could see anyone in a place of eternal misery and could hear their pleas for mercy, heaven would be hell to me unless God changed me into a cruel, merciless monster just as He is presented to be by the traditional creed. No thanks! As Thomas Allin has so eloquently put it, "Fancy a mother thrilled through with bliss while (near, or far off, it matters not) her child is in the grip of devils; a wife joining in the angelic harmonies, while her husband forever blasphemes!"

Listen to what I believe is the truly Christian attitude believers should have toward those who have not yet found our Savior in these words:

The Poet at the Breakfast Table

> What if a soul redeemed, a spirit that loved
> While yet on earth, and was beloved in turn,
> And still remembered every look and tone
> Of that dear earthly sister, who was left
> Among the unwise virgins at the gate:
> Itself admitted with the bridegroom's train—
> What if this spirit redeemed, amid the host
> Of chanting angels, in some transient lull
> Of the eternal anthem, heard the cry
> Of its lost darling, whom in evil hour
> Some wilder pulse of nature led astray,
> And left an outcast in a world of fire,
> Condemned to be the sport of cruel fiends,
> Sleepless, unpitying, masters of the skill
> To wring the maddest ecstasies of pain,
> From worn out souls that only ask to die—
> Would it not long to leave the bliss of heaven,
> Bearing a little water in its hand,
> To moisten those poor lips that plead in vain;
> With Him we call our Father?
>
> —Oliver Wendall Holmes

The popular creed actually teaches men to think lightly of sin. This may seem contradictory, but think about it. If God permits the existence of sin for all eternity in hell, what idea does that really convey to us? The toleration of sin! Have you ever thought about this? Nothing so effectively teaches men to bear with sin as the popular creed, because it teaches that God will bear with the existence of sin forever, even if it is tucked away in the "outer darkness," as a constant reminder of God's failure to save mankind and eradicate sin!

Another objection to eternal hell is that it punishes finite sins with infinite punishment. Where is the justice in that? Take the most heinous sins such as murder, rape, child abuse, genocide, and terrorism. No Christian would deny that any of these sins can be forgiven if the perpetrator merely receives Jesus Christ as his or her Lord and Savior. If all these sins can be forgiven in this life, why not in the life to come? Why should anyone be punished for all eternity for sins committed in time? Think about how long eternity is. Can you imagine anyone being tormented on and on and on and on!!!! If punishment is not meant for the reformation of the sinner, what else is it but pure, sadistic vindictiveness! Even annihilation as awful as that is would be far more just and far more in keeping with God's purpose in sending Jesus, stated in John 1:29: "Behold, the Lamb of God, who takes away the sin of the world!" In the traditional view, the sins of the majority of mankind are never taken away! They're just thrown into the eternal torture chamber called hell, where they fester and rot, getting worse and worse throughout eternity, an eternal testimony to the failure of God!

Jesus said something that surely reflects the character of God, since as all Evangelicals agree, Jesus is Himself God. He said in Luke 6:27–36:

> But I say to you who hear, Love your enemies, do good to those who hate you, bless those who curse you, pray for those who abuse you. To one who strikes you on the cheek, offer the other also, and from one who takes away your cloak do not withhold your tunic either. Give to everyone who begs from you, and from one who takes away your goods do not demand them back. And as you wish that others would do to you, do so to them.
>
> If you love those who love you, what benefit is that to you? For even sinners love those who love them. And if you do good to those who do good to you, what benefit is that to you? For even sinners do the same. And if you lend to those from whom you expect to receive, what credit is that to you? Even

sinners lend to sinners, to get back the same amount. But love your enemies, and do good, and lend, expecting nothing in return, and your reward will be great, and you will be sons of the Most High, for he is kind to the ungrateful and the evil. Be merciful, even as your Father is merciful.

Let's compare the God of eternal torment with this description of how God wants us to be. Does this God love His enemies? No way! You can't love someone and allow that person to be tormented forever! Does He do good to those who hate Him? Not unless you consider everlasting torment to be good! Does He give to everyone who begs from Him? No again. Where was God when the rich man in Hades asked Abraham for a drop of water? Does the God of eternal hell treat others as He wishes to be treated? I doubt He wants to go to hell! Is He merciful? Not unless condemning His own children to everlasting weeping, wailing, and gnashing of teeth can be considered merciful! The God of eternal hell is a hypocrite! He holds sinners to a far higher standard than He does for Himself. I am not mocking God. I am mocking a hideous parody of God! God is love! God is kind, compassionate, merciful, and forgiving. Yes, He is just. But His justice doesn't wipe out all of His other qualities!

CHAPTER 3

Why Endless Torment?

Out of the anguish of his soul he shall see and be satisfied. (Isaiah 53:11)

If you are a parent who loves your children, I would like to ask you a question: Do you ever punish your children? Of course you do. My next question is, Why? Is it just to inflict pain or is it to correct bad behavior? Would you ever reach a point where your children made you so mad you would just want to hurt them without any thought for whether or not it is in their best interest?

Do you think you love your children more than God loves His? If not, then how can you believe that God could ever give up on trying to save His children and order His angels to bind them hand and foot and cast them into a place of eternal torment?

Endless torment contradicts the true end of punishment, even apart from the question of its injustice. Apart from the horror it excites, it is useless. It is just pure sadistic, cruel barbarity, because it is only vindictive and is in no sense remedial. There is something positively sickening in the thought of the cruelty combined with the uselessness of a penalty prolonged, after all hope of repentance is over, and every sin being punished again, and again, and again simply for punishment's sake, shocking every sentiment of justice, especially when it is really the prolonging of evil. Jesus came to take away the sin of the world, not to make it last for all eternity in hell.

Matthew 25 is a favorite text of those who believe in eternal punishment. It is the story of the separation of the sheep (believers) and the goats (unbelievers). Verse 46 says in the English Standard Version, "And these [the goats] will go away into eternal punishment, but the righteous into eternal life." On the surface, this text seems to prove conclusively that there is indeed eternal punishment waiting for those who die unsaved. But, let's look a little closer. The Greek word translated "eternal" here is *aionios,* a form of the word *aion,* which is often translated as "age" in the New Testament, and in many places as it is used it cannot possibly mean everlasting. And the word translated "punishment" is not *timoria,* the word usually used to denote penalty or vengeance, but the word *kolasis,* which usually means "pruning" or "correction." Rotherham's *Emphasized Bible,* which is a literal word-for-word translation, renders it this way: "And [these] shall go away, into [age-abiding] correction, but [the righteous] into [age-abiding] life." This translation is certainly more in keeping with the central theme of the Bible, which is God's love for sinners!

Another thing I want to look at in regard to the doctrine of everlasting hell is its apparent pettiness or unworthiness of God. Even if we forget the fact that the Bible portrays God as good, righteous, and loving, if we imagine Him simply as great and mighty, it is difficult to picture this great Being attempting to save all of mankind and falling so short of His goal. He puts forth every effort to save mankind. He sends prophets to teach mankind about Him. He works miracles, signs, and wonders in heaven and earth. Finally, He sends His own Son, God in human form, who gives us a perfect example to follow, and then He allows Himself to be mocked, beaten, and nailed to a cross to save mankind. And what is the result according to the traditional creed? Only a pitifully few receive Him as their Lord and Savior. The rest are destined for eternal torment too terrible to even imagine, despite God's best effort to save them.

Jesus died for all men according to 2 Corinthians 5:14, "For the love of Christ controls us, because we have concluded this: that one [Christ] died for all, therefore all have died." Of course the New Testament is full of passages that teach that Jesus died for everyone, but the proponents of everlasting hell would have us believe that for the majority of mankind, Jesus died in vain.

Isaiah 53:11 says, "Out of the anguish of his soul he shall see and be satisfied." Will He be satisfied to see that His death for all men was a failure? Or that out of the billions of precious souls He gave His life for, only a tiny fraction will be saved and the rest will be tormented forever? To me it is inconceivable that God's plan to save the world should end in failure—that this would be the result of the agony of the eternal Son. The advocates of everlasting hell would have us believe that God Almighty devised a plan before the foundation of the world to save mankind and sent His only begotten Son to accomplish His plan by dying on the cross, and yet for most of mankind, His plan was a colossal failure. I can understand people who deny the deity of Christ, believing in His defeat; but it is incredible that those who believe Him to be God Almighty are the loudest in asserting His failure.

If we think of God worthily at all, we can't help thinking of Him as working for high and worthy ends. But what end does the popular creed assign to Him? It presents a creation ending in misery and endless sin for millions of those He created in His own image. And all of this misery and horror are made clearer by a vain and fruitless attempt to save all, by a purpose of love declared for all that actually reaches only a few, a creation that is just an entryway into endless sin and misery in hell for millions who have already suffered in this life. The Bible speaks of the morning stars singing together and the sons of God shouting for joy on the morning of creation. They should have wept if the popular creed is true, because that creed represents this present life as darkened by the prospect of evil triumphing over good. All of our present sorrows are increased by the prospect of a future life that will be not only to the lost but to all men a curse, a life that every good man would, if he could, bring to an instant end.

Why do I say that hell is a curse not only to the lost but to all men? If you are a parent, wouldn't you honestly rather that all men would cease to exist than for one of your precious children to go to a place of eternal torment? If we would think that way in the case of our own children, we are morally bound to make the same choice for everyone. No moral being, no one with an ounce of compassion, would consent to purchase eternal happiness at the price of another's eternal misery. Hence it follows that eternal hell would be a curse to all men.

CHAPTER 4

Eternal Hell? Unbelievable!

I will not be angry forever. (Jeremiah 3:12)

There is another very serious obstacle to accepting the popular creed. Nobody really believes it! Or at least they act as if they don't. If Christians really believed it not just as doctrine but in their hearts, if they had any compassion for their fellow man, they would not be able to rest, day or night, as long as one sinner remained who was lost. They would sacrifice everything—pleasure, learning, business, art, literature, golf, movies, everything. For a Christian who really believes that most of those around him are heading for eternal torture and misery, banished forever from the presence of God, to do anything else but try every waking moment to save them is like a fireman playing golf while his city is in flames. Don't ask me to believe that any human being who is convinced that his own child, his wife, his neighbor, or even his enemy is in danger of endless torment could, if really persuaded of this, live as men now live! If Christians really believed that the majority of the world was on its way to eternal hell, every believer would be like the Apostle Paul with no other interests but the salvation of souls. There wouldn't be any Christians going to the movies, watching TV, or playing golf. They would spend every moment warning people to get right with God! But is this the case? You know as well as I do that the answer is a resounding NO!!

No one lives as if he really believes that all around him are millions of people heading for eternal hell without a chance of escape without hearing and accepting the message that he possesses! It is impossible! Who would dare so much as to smile if he really believed that a member of his household was headed for a place of unending, unspeakable anguish and pain? Marriage would be a crime; every birth would be an occasion of awful dread. It is positively immoral to bring a new life into this world if you believed that child could possibly end up being tortured forever! To perpetuate the human race would be to perpetuate endless misery for millions of souls. If people really believed in everlasting hell, the world would be a madhouse!

To illustrate further that no one really believes this horrible doctrine, look at the way people act at funerals. A man dies, a nice guy, a decent man by worldly standards, but not a Christian. According to the popular creed, he has gone to hell forever. But who REALLY believes that? Instinctively, our words grow softer when we speak of the dead. Do even pastors really believe what they profess? If they do, why are they so often silent? It would be impossible for anyone who really believed in everlasting torment to stay silent!

How few even of those who are baptized and attend church regularly are really born again! They are nice people. Like all of us, they are not good enough for heaven, but neither are they bad enough for hell. Everywhere you look in churches and out, you will find good people, unselfish parents, hard workers, loving brothers and sisters, and true friends, and everywhere traces, even among all the sin, of goodness and self-sacrifice, sometimes even carried to great lengths. In times of sickness or emergency, there are non-Christians there ready to lend a helping hand. But according to the traditional doctrine of hell, all of those nice people are going to hell forever right alongside murderers, rapists, child molesters, and the worst sinners, and this is supposed to be part of the good news for all men! Any other creed or no creed at all would be a relief from this awful, false Gospel.

Another obstacle to belief in endless hell is the fact that wherever human beings exist, there is found a deep spontaneous belief—

call it feeling or instinct or whatever you want—that makes people rejoice at weddings and new births. Why is this? Is there no meaning? Surely such a deep instinct comes from God the Father of all! It is His voice that bids the bridegroom to rejoice over his bride, that bids the mother's heart to overflow with love and tenderness toward her baby. Is it possible that our Heavenly Father would bid His children everywhere to rejoice at the marriage feast or at the birth of a baby if these births were destined to add to the number of those destined to suffer forever in hell? If you say that the joy experienced at a new birth is instinct, that just proves that it comes from God. Would God plant within us the instinct to rejoice whenever children are born if most of them were destined for everlasting torment?

CHAPTER 5

We Were All Made for Heaven

You have made us for Yourself, and our hearts are restless until they find rest in You. (St. Augustine)

Another reason eternal hell doesn't make sense is the longing for happiness that God has placed within every one of us. If we are not all destined for happiness, why did God put the longing for it in our hearts? To mock us? If the doctrine of eternal torment is true, what a mockery it would be for God to place poor wretches on earth where they hear the happy shouts of children and the joyous song of birds, where they are surrounded by the beauty of the stars above and the dazzling array of colorful flowers below. If millions of people are born to be surrounded by beauty for a short time only to end up in a horrible place of terror, wickedness, and anguish, being tortured by demons forever, it would be like placing objects of beauty in the waiting room of a torture chamber.

C.S. Lewis says,

> The Christian says, "Creatures are not born with desires unless satisfaction for those desires exists. A baby feels hunger: well, there is such a thing as food. A duckling wants to swim: well, there is such a thing as water. Men feel sexual desire: well, there is such a thing as sex. If I find in myself a desire which no

experience in this world can satisfy, the most probable explanation is that I was made for another world. If none of my earthly pleasures satisfy it, that does not prove that the universe is a fraud. Probably earthly pleasures were never meant to satisfy it, but only to arouse it, to suggest the real thing. If that is so, I must take care, on the one hand, never to despise, or be unthankful for, these earthly blessings, and on the other, never to mistake them for the something else of which they are only a kind of copy, or echo, or mirage. I must keep alive in myself the desire for my true country, which I shall not find till after death; I must never let it get snowed under or turned aside; I must make it the main object of life to press on to that other country. And to help others do the same."

Consider also the vast potential for growth in every person. Does it really make sense for all of that potential to be lost at a person's death?

Look at nature, which is, according to Paul, a revelation of God. In nature, things develop in stages, yet we are told to believe that all opportunity for growth and change for discipline, repentance, and reformation are limited to our brief life here. To teach that the mere fact of dying is the signal for a total change from all that has gone before contradicts all that we know of God's ways. Consider this, and tell me that it makes sense to place so wide a gulf, as the commonly held view does between our present and future lives. In all of God's dealings with us, no sharp break intervenes between the successive stages of life. Infancy gradually turns into toddlerhood, which flows into adolescence, etc. This being true, can I believe that in the age to come this will all be reversed, and that people, with capacities for good still existing, are to be at once bound, consigned to hopeless sin and endless torture? Man is to live forever. It doesn't make sense that the few fleeting moments of our life here on earth should determine whether we spend eternity in endless joy or endless misery. God is longsuffering. Does His patience really run out so quickly?

If we look around us, it appears that this brief, present life is rather the initial stage of human training than its conclusion. The vast majority of men throughout history haven't even heard of Christ. Many die in infancy, some are developmentally disabled, others suffer from psychiatric problems, many are uneducated, and still others grow up in other religions where their minds are prejudiced against the Gospel. Are these millions to first hear of the lives they could have lived only before they are thrown into everlasting hell? I admit that many who believe in eternal hell believe that God will make exceptions in some of the cases above, but that still leaves millions upon millions of people who have never had an adequate opportunity to hear and respond to the Gospel.

Next consider how contradictory it would be for a religion to promote mercy, goodness, love, and compassion more than any other religion or system of belief, and at the same time teach that this loving God, whose very essence is love, will throw unbelievers into an everlasting torture chamber more cruel and sadistic than anything that even the cruelest criminal could ever conceive of, let alone carry out?

Usually when Christians evangelize, they try to convince sinners of the great loss to themselves. They tell them such things as "If you don't receive Christ as your Savior, you will lose your soul and be cast into hell." In the parables of the lost sheep and the lost coin, God is the one who will suffer loss if He doesn't find every last one of His sheep and bring them safely into His fold.

Look at Luke 15, verse 6: "And when he comes home, he calls together his friends and his neighbors, saying to them, 'Rejoice with me, for I have found my sheep that was lost.'"

Look at the story of the woman who had ten coins and lost one. If I were to lose a coin, I probably wouldn't bother looking too hard for it. I would figure, "Oh well. There are plenty more where that came from." But apparently these ten coins were all she had, and she was desperate to find the one she had lost. We read in verse 9: "And when she has found it, she calls together her friends and neighbors, saying, 'Rejoice with me, for I have found the coin that I had lost.'"

Look next at the story of the father who never gives up on His children. Read this in verse 20: "And he [the younger son] arose and came to his father. But while he was still a long way off, his father saw him and felt compassion, and ran and embraced him and kissed him." Does that father sound like the god of tradition, who arbitrarily sets death as the end of all chance for reconciliation? The father in the story, who of course represents God, has been waiting and watching for the return of his son, and when he sees him a long way off, he forgets all about decorum and peels out in a race with his son to see who can reach the other first. Is a God who loves His children more than any earthly father going to give up on them just because they die? Just think of the value He places on each one of us! He has created each of us in His own image! Can He destroy creatures made in His own image? Or even worse, could He give them over to be tortured forever? Would He send His only begotten Son to die for the sins of the whole world and then eternally damn most of those for whom that precious blood was shed?

CHAPTER 6

All Shall Live in Christ!

For as in Adam all die, so also in Christ shall all be made alive. (1 Corinthians 15:22)

The verse above, along with many others, teaches the organic unity of the entire human race. We have had two representatives. The first was Adam. When he sinned, he brought sin and death on the entire human race. None of us asked for him to represent us. None of us chose to be born as sinners doomed to die. But according to the verse above, that's the way it is, whether we like it or not. But that's not the end of the story. Jesus Christ, our second representative, has broken the curse of the Fall for all of us so that we shall all be made alive!

Some try to say that the second "all" in the verse means only believers, but that is pure sophistry or specious reasoning. You can't say that the first clause of the verse teaches the fall of all mankind in Adam without the second clause teaching the salvation of all mankind in Christ! It hardly makes sense that Paul would use the same word "all" in both clauses of the same sentence without meaning the same group of people in both clauses. If you look at any commentary on this verse, the writers don't even try to explain it. They just try to explain it away by quoting other verses that seem to contradict its clear teaching.

Look at Romans 5:18–19: "Therefore, as one trespass led to

condemnation for ALL men, so one act of righteousness leads to justification and life for ALL men. For as by the one man's disobedience the many [ALL people] were made sinners, so by the one man's obedience the many [ALL people] will be made righteous." Could words be any clearer? Why keep trying to explain away the most glorious truth in the Bible? God loves ALL men! Jesus died for ALL men! ALL men will finally be saved! Nowhere in the Bible does it say that Jesus is the potential Savior of all. He is the Savior of ALL!

1 Timothy 4:10 says, "We have our hope set on the living God, who is the Savior of all people, especially of those who believe." What does that last phrase mean? It probably means that those who believe now in this life are saved now, and the rest will be saved later. But one thing the verse clearly teaches is the salvation of ALL. Augustine was the first person we know of who tried to explain away this verse and others by saying that it means that God is the Savior of all kinds of people, not all people. That's not what it says. "God ... is the Savior of all people!"

This is illustrated by the firstfruits. In the Old Testament, the Jews were commanded to give the firstfruits of everything, signifying that everything belongs to the Lord. 1 Corinthians 15:20 says, "Christ has been raised from the dead, the firstfruits of those who have fallen asleep." This verse is clearly saying in context that Jesus rose from the dead as a guarantee that all of Adam's offspring will be raised. This is seen in the verse that heads this chapter, 1 Corinthians 15:22: "For as in Adam all die, so also in Christ shall all be made alive." In verse 23, Christ is again referred to as the firstfruits. It could be argued from verse 23 that Jesus is the firstfruits only of those who belong to Him at His coming. But the rest of the passage goes on to say that God has put all things in subjection under Jesus' feet and that when they are all subjected to Him, Jesus Himself will be subjected to the Father so that God may be all in all.

If there is an everlasting hell, the day of ALL things being subjected to God and God being "all in all" will never come! The enemies of God will be rebelling against God forever! This can never be. God will be "all in all" when ALL of His enemies have been turned into friends. This will be when, as it says in Revelation

5:13, "EVERY creature in heaven and on earth and under the earth and in the sea, and ALL that is in them, (are) saying, 'To him who sits on the throne and to the Lamb be blessing and honor and glory and might forever and ever!'"

CHAPTER 7

The Immutability of God

I the Lord do not change. (Malachi 3:6)

The traditional view is clearly in contradiction to the clear teaching of God's Word that God is unchanging! If He loves all of His children now, He will always love them. Allowing any of them to go to a place of unending torment would be a sign of hatred, not love!

Thomas Allin tells a story that he says actually happened that shows the absurdity of a loving God abandoning any of His children to everlasting hell. In a certain place in London, an evangelist had just preached an evangelistic message when one of his listeners asked him, "Sir, may I ask you one or two questions?" When the evangelist answered in the affirmative, the man said, "You have told us that God's love for us is very great and very strong and that He sent His Son to save us, and that I may be saved this moment, if I will. But if I go away without an immediate acceptance of this offer, and if a few minutes later I am killed by an accident on my way home, I would find myself in hell for ever and ever." The evangelist answered, "Yes." The man then said, "If that is true, I don't want anything to do with a being whose love for me can change so completely in five minutes."

John 3:16: "For God so loved the world, that he gave his only Son, that whoever believes in him should not perish but have eternal life." Look at that little two-letter word "so." It speaks volumes.

Let's change this verse a little and see if it makes sense: "For God so loved the world that if any of them do not believe in his Son, he will throw them into everlasting torment." Does that make sense? That's what the traditional view teaches: In spite of His great love for mankind, anyone who does not believe in Him in this life will be thrown by Him into a place that makes the torture chambers of the Inquisition look like Disneyland forever! No! The God who *so* loves the world will always love them because He is unchanging.

To say that God is unchanging is to say that His love is unchanging. His love will pursue sinners even into the outer darkness and draw them from there back to Himself. An earthly parent who is able to help yet chooses to sit unmoved month after month, year after year, watching the agonies of his own offspring, but never helping, is a picture more hideous than any records of crime can furnish. What can we say of those who make the scenario infinitely worse by making the father in the story God who is love?

This brings us face to face with a radical blunder of the traditional creed. It talks of God's love as though it stood merely on a par with His justice as if it were something belonging to Him that He puts on or off. It is hardly possible to open a religious book in which this fatal error isn't found. It is fatal because it virtually strikes out of the Gospel its fundamental truth that God is love! The Bible never says, "God is justice," though He is just. It never says, "God is vengeance," though He does avenge. Those are attributes. Love is God's essence. It's who He is! God is not loving at one moment and just the next. His justice is loving justice. Where is the love in abandoning His children to eternal torment? The traditional creed knows nothing of what love really is. If it did, it would see God first and foremost as a loving Father, not a judge. It would see that the Gospel is first and foremost the story of a Father who longs to be reconciled with all of His wayward children rather than a King who is angry with His subjects. Yes, God will judge. But to put more emphasis on His judgment than on His grace is a distortion of the Gospel.

Hebrews 13:8: "Jesus Christ is the same yesterday, today, and forever." He loves all of us now, and He always will!

CHAPTER 8

Universalism in Church History

*When death shall no longer exist, or the sting of death,
nor any evil at all, then, truly, God will be all in all.
(Origen)*

"If Universalism is scriptural, why hasn't anybody in the history of Christianity ever believed it?" The fact is that they have. When the doctrine of justification by grace through faith alone was rediscovered a little over four hundred years ago after being obscured for centuries, people could have asked the same thing they ask now about Universalism.

In 1521, Martin Luther was called before the Council, then known as the Diet, of the town of Worms to answer for his "heretical" views, particularly the outlandish idea that believers are justified by grace through faith alone. When he was asked to retract his teachings, he replied, "Unless I am convinced by scripture or by clear reason—for I do not trust the Pope or Church councils, since everyone knows they can make mistakes and contradict themselves—I am bound by the scriptures I have quoted. My conscience is held captive by the Word of God. I cannot and will not take back anything, because it is neither safe nor right to go against conscience. Here I stand, I can do no other. God help me. Amen."

Whatever you think of Luther, you've got to admit it took guts for him to stand up for scripture against the established church. Jonathan Hill says in his book *The History of Christian Thought*, "The emperor declared that if one monk stood against the whole of Christendom, then he must be wrong, for it was unthinkable that the entire church could have been wrong for the past 1,000 years. He condemned Luther as a heretic."

Ever since the doctrine of everlasting hell became the official teaching of the church hundreds of years after its founding by our Lord Jesus Christ, there have been brave souls who have stood up for the clear scriptural teaching of God's love for all men and His intention to save all men. Just because they were going against the beliefs of the majority in the church does not make them wrong any more than Luther was wrong to teach salvation by grace through faith alone. Truth is truth, no matter who believes it and who does not. Just because people have temporarily lost sight of a truth doesn't make it any less true!

I will now attempt to show that the belief in the eventual salvation of all men is a belief that was widely held in the early Church. Indeed, as I have said, there is evidence that this was the majority view for at least the first four to five centuries of the Church. Most of the earliest Church Fathers—those who came directly after the Apostles and for whom Greek, the language the New Testament was written in, was their primary language—believed that because God is not willing that any should perish but that all should come to repentance, and that no one can thwart God's will, that all would in fact be saved. It is a striking fact that most of the opposition to Universalism in primitive times is found in the Latin Church and, as in Augustine's case, where the Greek language was never really mastered.

Before we can hope to understand the Fathers or to rightly estimate the force of their testimony, we have to try to mentally put ourselves into their place. The Church was born into a world of moral rottenness that we can little imagine. The foulest lusts and debauchery raged on every side. To assert the final salvation of all in such a moral climate necessitated a firm belief that this was indeed the teaching of Scripture. The Church was engaged in a life and death struggle for survival. Believers were relentlessly persecuted and cruelly tortured and killed for their faith. To teach the salvation of all must have seemed like treason to some. To teach that even their cruel, unrepentant persecutors should yet find salvation in the ages to come doesn't seem to be something they would have taught unless they firmly believed it to be the testimony of Scripture. Such considerations should make us willing to give a lot of weight to the smallest expressions of this teaching in their writings.

There is a very early writing called the Gospel of Nicodemus from the second century that, though not canonical, is instructive. The writer, taking his cue from 1 Peter 3:19, which speaks of Christ preaching to the spirits in prison, expands on this dramatically. In it, a great voice echoes through Hades crying, "Lift up your heads, ye gates, and the King of glory shall come in." Immediately the gates are shattered! And all of those bound come out! Hades personified exclaims, "Not one of the dead has been left in me." Jesus then turns to Adam, extending His right hand and raising him. Then Jesus says to the rest, "Come with me! All of you who have died because of the tree Adam touched, for behold I raise you all up through the tree of the cross."

Another ancient book called the Acts of the Apostle Thomas addresses Christ as the Savior of every creature: "You who went down even to Hades, and brought out from there those shut in for many ages."

Origen, commenting on Psalm 68:18, "You ascended on high, leading a host of captives in your train," says, "Christ raised up and set free from the recesses of Hades, the souls that were held in captivity."

In a passage that is ascribed to Athanasius, it says, "While the devil thought to kill one he is deprived of all ... cast out of Hades, sitting by the gates, he sees all the fettered beings led forth by the courage of the Savior."

Didymus in 370 A.D. writes, "In the liberation of all no one remains a captive! At the time of the Lord's passion the devil alone was injured by losing all of the captives he was keeping."

St. Ambrose, 375 A.D., writes, "The Lord descends to the infernal world, in order that even those, who were in the infernal abodes, should be set free from their perpetual bonds."

St. Chrysostom, 398 A.D., writes "While the devil imagined that he got hold of Christ, he really lost all of those he was keeping."

Cyril of Alexandria, 412 A.D., describes Christ as having emptied Hades, and "left the devil there solitary and deserted."

Theodoret, 430 A.D., said that Christ said to the devil, "I'm going to open the prison of death for the rest, but shut you up alone."

All of these quotes, and many more that could be adduced, seem to be commenting on 1 Peter 3:19, which says that Christ "went and proclaimed to the spirits in prison." What did He proclaim, and who were these spirits He proclaimed it to? 1 Peter 4:6 gives the answer to both questions: "The gospel was preached even to those who are dead, that though judged in the flesh the way people are, they might live in the spirit the way God does." Commentators and preachers go to great lengths to explain away the clear teaching of these passages, but the early Christians knew exactly what they were saying. If they were right, if Christ delivered from Hades every soul of Adam's race up to the time of His crucifixion, if every murderer, every blasphemer, and every adulterer, though dying unrepentant, was at last evangelized and saved by Christ, then on what grounds can it be fairly or reasonably asserted that less mercy will be extended to the rest of our race whose only difference is that they were born later?

For many years after the apostolic days, there is a scarcity of records of Christian thought, but some of the writings that are no longer extant are quoted from or alluded to in other writings that are still in existence. Pamphilus the martyr, 294 A.D., in conjunction with Eusebius, wrote an Apology for Origen that is no longer in existence. Two very early anonymous writers agree in stating that this work contained very many testimonies of Fathers earlier than Origen in favor of universal restitution. Origen was born about ninety years after the death of the Apostle John. This would obviously mean that this teaching was believed in by many Christian writers dating very far back.

Clement of Alexandria, 190 A.D., who speaks of having learned from a disciple of the Apostles, clearly taught the salvation of all. The following are quotes from his writings:

> All men are Christ's, some by knowing Him, the rest not yet.
>
> He is the Savior, not of some and of the rest not.
>
> For how is He Lord and Savior if He is not Lord and Savior of all?
>
> But He is indeed Savior of those who believe ... while of those who do not believe He is Lord, until having become able to confess Him, they obtain through Him the benefits appropriate and suitable [to their case].
>
> He by the Father's will directs the salvation of all. ... For all things have been ordered, both universally and in part, by the Lord of the universe, with a view to the salvation of the universe.
>
> If in this life there are so many ways for purification and repentance, how much more should there be after death! The purification of souls, when separated from the body, will be easier. We can set no limits to the agency of the Redeemer to redeem, to rescue, to discipline, is His work, and so will He continue to operate after this life.

Next I'll give a few quotes from the famous Origen, 234 A.D., born in Alexandria and called at the age of eighteen to preside over its school of theology. Commenting on 1 Corinthians 15:28, which reads, "When all things are subjected to him, then the Son himself will also be subjected to him who put all things in subjection under him, that God may be all in all," Origen said, "When the Son is said to be subject to the Father, the perfect restoration of the whole creation is signified." He goes on to say:

> When death shall no longer exist, or the sting of death, nor any evil at all, then, truly, God will be all in all.
>
> We assert that the Word, who is the wisdom of God, shall bring together all intelligent creatures, and convert them into His own perfection, through

> the instrumentality of their free will and of their own exertions. The Word is more powerful than all the diseases of the soul, and He applies His remedies to each one according to the pleasure of God, for the name of God is to be invoked by all, so that all shall serve Him with one consent.
>
> The end and consummation of the world will take place, when ALL shall be subjected to punishments proportioned to their several sins; and how long each one shall suffer, in order to receive his deserts, God only knows. But we suppose that the goodness of God, through Christ, will certainly restore ALL creatures into one final state; His very enemies being over come and subdued.

A pastor friend once implied to me that we shouldn't give any credence to Origen because he was condemned as a heretic by the early church. Actually the church that condemned him was not the pure church of Jesus Christ; it was the Roman Catholic Church that had already become corrupted by unbiblical teachings and practices. Origen's teachings about universal salvation were not condemned until 553 A.D.(almost three hundred years after his death) under the emperor Justinian, who persecuted those he considered heretics! In his own day, Origen was widely respected by the church, and not even those who disagreed with his views considered him a heretic. Jonathan Hill, in his book *The History of Christian Thought,* writes, "Origen is, together with Augustine and Luther, one of the most important figures in this book. Almost single-handedly the 'Iron Man,' as he was known, dragged Christianity into intellectual respectability. One of the greatest minds of his age, he debated with pagan philosophers as their superior. The systematic destruction of most of his writings after his death—by churchmen unworthy to inherit them—robbed the church of one of its greatest treasures. This tragic loss, together with the suspicion that still surrounds the name of Origen, has meant that that name has not received the praise due to it by the church at large."

Diodore of Tarsus, 320–394 A.D., wrote: "For the wicked there are punishments, not perpetual, however, lest the immortality prepared for them should be a disadvantage, but they are to be purified for a brief period according to the amount of malice in their works. They shall therefore suffer punishment for a short space, but immortal blessedness having no end awaits them ... the penalties to be inflicted for their many and grave sins are very far surpassed by the magnitude of the mercy to be showed them."

Macrina, 327–379: "The process of healing shall be proportioned to the measure of evil in each of us, and when the evil is purged and blotted out, there shall come in each place to each immortality and life and honor."

Gregory of Nazianzus, 330–390: "Let them, if they will, walk in our way and in Christ's. If not, let them walk in their own way. Maybe there they will be baptized with fire, with that last, that more laborious and longer baptism, which devours the substance like hay, and consumes the lightness of all evil." He seems to be alluding to 1 Corinthians 3:12–15: "Now if anyone builds on the foundation [Jesus] with gold, silver, precious stones, wood, hay, straw—each one's work will become manifest, for the Day will disclose it, because it will be revealed by fire, and the fire will test what sort of work each has done. If the work that anyone has built on the foundation survives, he will receive a reward. If anyone's work is burned up, he will suffer loss, though he himself will be saved, but only as through fire."

St. Jerome, 331–420: "In the end and consummation of the Universe all are to be restored into their original harmonious state, and we all shall be made one body and be united once more into a perfect man, and the prayer of our Savior shall be fulfilled that all may be one."

St. Gregory of Nyssa, 335–390: "For it is evident that God will in truth be 'in all' when there shall be no evil in existence, when every created being is at harmony with itself, and every tongue shall confess that Jesus Christ is Lord; when every creature shall have been made one body. Now the body of Christ, as I have often said, is the whole of humanity. ... Participation in bliss awaits everyone."

Theodore of Mopsuestia, 350–428: "The wicked who have

committed evil the whole period of their lives shall be punished till they learn that, by continuing in sin, they only continue in misery. And when, by this means, they shall have been brought to fear God, and to regard Him with good will, they shall obtain the enjoyment of His grace."

Theodoret the Blessed, 387–458: "In the present life God is in all, for His nature is without limits, but is not all in all. But in the coming life, when mortality is at an end and immortality granted, and sin has no longer any place, God will be all in all. For the Lord, who loves man, punishes medicinally, that He may check the course of impiety."

Peter Chrysologus, 435: "That in the world to come, those who have done evil all their life long, will be made worthy of the sweetness of the Divine bounty. For never would Christ have said, 'You will never get out until you have paid the last penny' unless it were possible for us to be cleansed when we have paid the debt."

St. Basil the Great, 329–379, wrote, "The mass of men say there is to be an end of punishment to those who are punished."

Augustine, 354–430: "Some—indeed very many—yield to merely human feelings and deplore the notion of the eternal punishment of the damned and their interminable and perpetual misery. They do not believe that such things will be. Not that they would go counter to Scripture—but yielding to their own human feelings, they soften what seems harsh and give a milder emphasis to statements they believe are meant more to terrify than to express literal truth."

Augustine speaks of "merely human feelings," as if it is natural for men to be tenderhearted but God is tougher. Rather, it is those who yield to human feelings who are imitating and obeying God. Ephesians 4:32: "Be kind to one another, tenderhearted, forgiving one another, as God in Christ forgave you." Thank God that He is more tenderhearted than Augustine!

CHAPTER 9

Universalism and Creation

Adam, the Son of God. (Luke 3:28)

Why did God create mankind? God, who is omniscient (all-knowing), knew before He ever created man that Adam and Eve would disobey Him and bring sin and death on all men. He also knew that if He provided a way of salvation, not all men—indeed, very few—would avail themselves of it, at least in this life. In short, He knew that creating mankind would be a disaster if human history on this earth is any indicator. So why did He do it? Would a loving God create people with full knowledge that the vast majority of them would end up in everlasting hell?

Of course, God is infinite and we are finite and we cannot expect to fully understand His ways, but He has created us with some intelligence, some ability to reason. Does it seem at all reasonable that God would create people as objects of His love and then allow most of them to end up as objects of eternal wrath? Even allowing for the possibility that there will be more in heaven than in hell, the question remains: Would a loving God create ANYONE knowing that his or her destiny is eternal torment? We will find—and the fact is a striking confirmation of Universalism—that all of the great truths of our faith come together into a living unity in the light of God's plan for the restoration of all things as promised in Acts 3:21: "[Jesus], whom heaven must receive until the time for restoring all the things about which God spoke by the mouth of his holy prophets long ago."

The Bible begins with the story of creation. In Colossians 1:16–20, the themes of creation and restoration are closely linked. In verses 16–19, it tells about the fact that all things were created through Christ and for Christ and how all the fullness of God was pleased to dwell in Christ. Then in verses 19 and 20, it speaks of how God was pleased to reconcile ALL things in heaven and on earth to Himself through Christ, who made peace by the blood of His cross. When God created mankind, it was with full knowledge of the Fall, but it was also with a foolproof plan for the restoration and reconciliation of all things to Himself so that "every knee should bow, in heaven and on earth and under the earth, and every tongue confess that Jesus Christ is Lord, to the glory of God the Father" (Philippians 2:10–11).

CHAPTER 10

What The Old Testament Teaches

*The whole history of the world is the uninterrupted
carrying through of a divine plan of salvation; the
primary object of which is His people: in and with them
however also the whole of humanity.
(Delitzech on Psalm 33:11)*

In Acts 3: 21, Peter says that the Lord will send Jesus, "whom heaven must receive until the time for restoring all the things about which God spoke by the mouth of his holy prophets long ago."

In looking at this verse in many different translations, the ESV does not seem to have the best translation. The NASB translates it this way: "Whom heaven must receive until the period of restoration of all things about which God spoke by the mouth of His holy prophets from ancient time."

The difference is subtle, but by adding the word "the" between the words "all" and "things," the ESV seems to be referring to the restoration of certain things while the NASB and all of the other translations I studied speak of the restoration of all things, or as the NIV has it, of "everything."

Universalists believe that this restoration Peter is speaking of involves no less than the salvation of all men, and that Peter was reiterating something that God had said through His prophets many times.

In Genesis 12:3, God promised Abraham, "In you all the families of the earth shall be blessed." This promise of a worldwide blessing grows more frequent as the stream of revelation flows on. There are clear traces of it in the Law, the Psalms, and the Prophets. In the Law was the teaching of the firstfruits and the firstborn, which has been pointed out earlier as being very significant in our study of universal salvation. As the firstfruits represent that the entire harvest belongs to God and the firstborn represents the whole family, God's chosen people are a pledge that all are God's, that all are destined to share His blessings. As firstfruits, they are the channels of blessing to all mankind:

> Psalm 22:27: "All the ends of the earth shall remember and turn to the Lord, and all the families of the nations shall worship before you."

> Psalm 24:1: "The earth is the Lord's and the fullness thereof, the world and those who dwell therein."

> Psalm 33:8: "Let all the earth fear the Lord; let all the inhabitants of the world stand in awe of him!"

> Psalm 67:3–4: "Let the peoples praise you, O God; let all the peoples praise you! Let the nations be glad and sing for joy, for you judge the peoples with equity and guide the nations upon earth."

> Psalm 68:32: "O kingdoms of the earth, sing to God; sing praises to the Lord."

> Psalm 69:34: "Let heaven and earth praise him, the seas and everything that moves in them."

> Psalm 72:11: "May all kings fall down before

him, all nations serve him!"

Psalm 86:9: "All the nations you have made shall come and worship before you, O Lord, and shall glorify your name."

Psalm 150:6: "Let everything that has breath praise the Lord! Praise the Lord!"

Of the major prophets from the midst of their various contents, at times promises break forth of the widest, fullest hope; anticipations of a time of universal bliss and joy; of a world in which all pain and sorrow have passed away.

Isaiah 45:22–23: "Turn to me and be saved, all the ends of the earth! For I am God, and there is no other. By myself I have sworn; from my mouth has gone out in righteousness a word that shall not return: To me every knee shall bow, every tongue shall swear allegiance." Could any words more emphatically declare that the divine purpose is that the whole earth, to its very end, shall be saved, or that every knee shall bow in worship before God and every tongue shall swear allegiance to Him? Aren't we told expressly that this declaration, since it has gone out from the righteous mouth of God, shall not return to Him without accomplishing its purpose—that object being the salvation of all mankind?

Paul echoes this great word in Romans 14:11 and in Philippians 2:9–11. Romans 14:11: "As I live, says the Lord, every knee shall bow to me, and every tongue shall confess to God." Philippians 2:9–11: "Therefore God has highly exalted him and bestowed on him the name that is above every name, so that at the name of Jesus every knee should bow, in heaven and earth and under the earth, and every tongue confess that Jesus Christ is Lord, to the glory of God the Father." People have told me that these passages don't teach that all men will be saved, but only that all will bow before Jesus, some willingly and some grudgingly. Surely the phrase "to the glory of God the Father" rules out such an interpretation. Jesus does not accept insincere praise. In Luke 4:41, we read, "And demons also came out of many, crying, 'You are the Son of God!' But he rebuked them and would not allow them to speak."

Acts 16:16–18: "As we [Paul and his companions] were going to the place of prayer, we were met by a slave girl who had a spirit of divination and brought her owners much gain by fortune-telling. She followed Paul and us, crying out, 'These men are servants of the Most High God, who proclaim to you the way of salvation.' And this she kept doing for many days. Paul, having become greatly annoyed, turned and said to the spirit, 'I command you in the name of Jesus Christ to come out of her.' And it came out that very hour." Why was Paul so annoyed? Wasn't what the girl said true?

Yes! But God doesn't want praise unless it comes from the right source and the right motives. 1 Corinthians 12:3 says, "No one can say 'Jesus is Lord' except in the Holy Spirit." How would it glorify God for the eternally damned to kneel before Jesus and proclaim Him as Lord before going off to hell? Their continued wickedness and rebellion in hell would just be an everlasting testimony to the fact that He had failed to conquer their hearts.

No! Isaiah 45:23, Romans 14:11, and Philippians 2:9–11 all testify to the fact that eventually the love of God will do what His power alone cannot do—conquer the hearts of His enemies and make them His willing servants.

Another passage that is similar to these makes this fact even clearer. Revelation 5:13: "And I [John] heard EVERY creature in heaven and on earth and under the earth and in the sea, and ALL that is in them, saying, 'To him who sits on the throne and to the Lamb be blessing and honor and glory and might forever and ever!'" Surely even the most prejudiced mind can see that this verse foresees a time when everybody everywhere will worship the Father and the Son!

This verse proves either universal salvation or annihilation of the lost. Either everyone has been converted or the lost have been annihilated, because John envisions a time when everybody everywhere is worshiping the Father and the Son.

The next verse I want to look at is Isaiah 53:11, which is a prophecy of the crucifixion of our Lord: "Out of the anguish of his soul he shall see and be satisfied." The New Living Translation puts it this way: "When he sees all that is accomplished by his anguish, he will be satisfied." If His goal in dying was the salvation of the world, will He really look at the pitifully few who are saved while on earth and be satisfied? Or wouldn't He be disappointed that the results of His death fell so short of His goal? Not if the rest will yet be saved.

How can I accept a creed that expects me to believe that Christ will be satisfied with the vast majority of those created in the very image of God being abandoned to everlasting torment!

Remember how full are the Prophets and the Psalms and all of God's Word of pictures of the vastness of divine mercy, of His tenderness that never fails!

Even in the midst of the sadness of the Lamentations, we hear a voice assuring us: "The Lord will not cast off forever, but, though he cause grief, he will have compassion according to the abundance of his steadfast love; for he does not willingly afflict or grieve the children of men" (Lamentations 3:31–33).

The Bible repeatedly states that God's wrath is very short lived but His mercy is everlasting:

> Isaiah 54:7–8: "'For a brief moment I deserted you, but with great compassion I will gather you. In overflowing anger for a moment I hid my face from you, but with everlasting love I will have compassion on you,' says the Lord, your Redeemer."

> Jeremiah 3:12: "I will not be angry forever."

> Psalm 30:5: "For his anger is but for a moment, and his favor is for a lifetime."

> Psalm 136 repeats the statement "his steadfast love endures forever" twenty-six times!

> Psalm 103:9–10: "He will not always chide, nor will he keep his anger forever. He does not deal with us according to our sins, nor repay us according to our iniquities."

Micah 7:18: "He does not retain his anger forever, because he delights in steadfast love."

How can this truth of the temporary nature of God's wrath be reconciled with the traditional creed that says that His wrath will endure forever?

Daniel 7:13–14: "Behold, with the clouds of heaven there came one like a son of man, and he came to the Ancient of Days and was presented before him. And to him was given dominion and glory and a kingdom, that all peoples, nations, and languages should serve him; his dominion is an everlasting dominion, which shall not pass away, and his kingdom one that shall not be destroyed." Jesus is the King of all people of all nations and all languages and as we saw in Revelation 5:13—everyone everywhere will worship Him.

In Daniel 9:24, the prophecy about the seventy weeks, we read that Jesus, the anointed one, will "put an end to sin." If the doctrine of everlasting hell is true, this part of Daniel's prophecy will never come true! Sin will continue to exist forever!

The Minor Prophets also look forward to the triumph of Christ.

In Hosea 13:14 we read, "O Death, where are your plagues? O Sheol, where is your sting?" Paul probably had this passage in mind when he wrote 1 Corinthians 15:55: "O death, where is your victory? O death, where is your sting?" If the doctrine of everlasting hell is true, death is indeed victorious in millions upon millions of cases.

Habakkuk 2:14: "For the earth will be filled with the knowledge of the glory of the Lord as the waters cover the sea."

CHAPTER 11

What the New Testament Teaches

God did not send his Son into the world to condemn the world, but in order that the world might be saved through him. (John 3:17)

We now turn to an examination of the many passages in the New Testament that clearly state or imply the salvation of ALL men. The time has come for boldly appealing to the letter and the spirit of the New Testament on behalf of the wider hope. I ask just one thing that common fairness and honesty require—that you try to put aside your preconceived ideas, try to keep an open mind, and let our Lord and His inspired spokesmen mean what they say.

When they speak of "all men," I assume them to mean all men, not some men. When they speak of "all things," I assume them to mean all things. When they speak of life and salvation as being for the whole world, I assume them to mean that they are not merely offered to the whole world but that the whole world will in fact be saved. When they speak of the destruction of sin and death and the works of the devil, I assume that ALL of these will be destroyed and not preserved forever in hell. When they tell us that Redemption is wider, broader, and stronger than the Fall, I assume that they mean that ALL of the evil consequences of the fall will be swept away. When they describe Christ's Kingdom extending over "all things" and "all creatures," and tell us that "*every* knee shall bow ... and *every* tongue confess that Jesus Christ is Lord" (Philippians 2:10–11) or that "EVERY creature in heaven and on earth and under the earth and in the sea, and ALL that is in them, (will be) saying, 'To him who sits on the throne and to the Lamb be blessing and honor and glory and might forever and ever!'" (Revelation 5:13) I assume these words to mean what they would mean in their ordinary sense.

I protest against teaching that "all" means "all" when it is talking about sin and death, but that "all" means only "some" when spoken of final salvation. The restoration of all things means, we are told, that only some beings are to be restored, while the rest are tortured forever or annihilated. That God will be "all in all" means that millions will be cast into hell forever to hate God and blaspheme Him forever and only a few will be saved. That His tender mercies are over all His works means, in the traditional creed, that His tender mercies expire at the gates of hell. It is ludicrous that those who believe in everlasting hell charge us with evading the words of Scripture.

I submit that the entire history of biblical interpretation contains no stranger fact than this persistent ignoring of such a large part of the New Testament.

To bring this out clearly, I'm going to quote from a number of texts that have been pieced together like the links of a chain that all fit together to show that the Kingdom of Christ will one day include everyone who has ever lived and God will truly be "all in all."

The chain begins at creation when all things were created by Christ with full knowledge of the fall of man that was to come and a plan already in place to redeem mankind. He who created all things will "reconcile to himself ALL things, whether on earth or in heaven, making peace by the blood of his cross" (Colossians 1:20). This reconciliation or restoration of ALL things was foretold by God when He "spoke by the mouth of his holy prophets long ago" (Acts 3:21). God has appointed His Son to be the "heir of ALL things" (Hebrews 1:2) and in God's Son "shall ALL the nations be blessed" (Galatians 3:8).

God has given His Son "authority over ALL flesh, to give eternal life to ALL whom He has given Him" (John 17:2). "The Father has given ALL things into the Son's hands" (John 3:35) and so "ALL flesh shall see the salvation of God" (Luke 3:6). Because of "the unchangeable character of God's purpose" (Hebrews 6:17), because His love for His enemies is unchanging and "He is kind to the ungrateful and evil" (Luke 6:35), "He desires ALL people to be saved" (1 Timothy 2:4). He "gave himself as a ransom for ALL" (1 Timothy 2:6). He "is not wishing that ANY should perish, but that ALL should reach repentance" (2 Peter 3:9). He "has consigned ALL to disobedience, that he may have mercy on ALL" (Romans 11:32) "for from him and through him and to him are ALL things" (Romans 11:36).

So God's plan is "to unite ALL things in Christ, things in heaven and things on earth" (Ephesians 1:10). The Father has "put ALL things under Christ's feet" (Ephesians 1:22) and has "given ALL things into his hands" (John 13:3). Jesus has promised to "draw ALL men" to Himself (John 12:32) because "the Father loves the Son and has given ALL things into his hand" (John 3:35). Jesus said, "ALL that the Father gives me will come to me" (John 6:37). Jesus says that like a good shepherd, He will search for each of His lost sheep "until he finds it" (Luke 15:4). "God did not send his Son into the world to condemn the world, but in order that the world might be saved through him" (John 3:37). "The grace of God has appeared bringing salvation for ALL people" (Titus 2:11).

Jesus is the "Lamb of God, who takes away the sin of the world" (John 1:29). Jesus gave His flesh as bread "for the life of the world" (John 6:51). "He gives life to the world" (John 6:33). He is "the light of the world" (John 8:12). "He is the propitiation for our sins, and not for ours only but also for the sins of the whole world" (1 John 2:2). "He is the Savior of ALL people" (1 Timothy 4:10). "He appeared to destroy the works of the devil" (1 John 3:8).

Jesus "abolished death" (2 Timothy 1:10). "He has put away sin by the sacrifice of himself" (Hebrews 9:26). His power "enables him to subject all things to himself" (Philippians 3:21). "The gospel was preached even to those who are dead, that though judged in the flesh the way people are, they might live in the spirit the way God does" (1 Peter 4:6). He has "the keys of Death and Hades" (Revelation 1:18). He will throw "Death and Hades into the lake of fire" (Revelation 20:14).

"In Christ shall all be made alive" (1 Corinthians 15:22). He "accomplished the work" that the Father gave Him to do (John 17:4). "He restores all things" (Acts 3:21). "At the name of Jesus every knee should bow, in heaven and earth and under the earth, and every tongue confess that Jesus Christ is Lord, to the glory of God the Father" (Philippians 2:10–11). "Every creature in heaven and on earth and under the earth and in the sea, and all that is in them, saying, 'To him who sits on the throne and to the Lamb be blessing and honor and glory and might forever and ever!'" (Revelation 5:13).

"Then comes the end, when he [Jesus] delivers the kingdom to God the Father after destroying every rule and every authority and power. For he must reign until he has put all his enemies under his feet. The last enemy to be destroyed is death. For 'God has put all things in subjection under his feet.' But when it says 'all things are put in subjection,' it is plain that he is excepted who put all things in subjection under him. When all things are subjected to him, then the Son himself will also be subjected to him who put all things in subjection under him, that God may be all in all" (1 Corinthians 15:24–28).

These verses have not just been thrown together haphazardly. They are the expression of that purpose that runs through the Bible, a purpose first stated in mankind's creation in the image of God, a purpose that can be traced throughout the entire Bible, in the Law, the Psalms, and the Prophets, and most clearly in the New Testament. From it we learn at least three things:

1. Christ came claiming the entire human race as His own, to the end that He would save and restore the entire race, not just part of it.
2. He came with full power and authority over all men, having received all power in heaven and earth over all hearts, all evil, all wills.
3. He lived and died and rose again, completely victorious,

having fully accomplished the work His Father gave Him to do, which was the salvation of the world.

To deny universal restoration and reconciliation is to mutilate the Scriptures. We are not dealing with a few isolated verses in which it might be possible to say that "all" was used loosely and doesn't really mean "all." We have a connected series in which link follows link—a series that teaches the actual, not potential, universality of Christ's Kingdom. Let's look closer at these passages, taking them in their natural and fair meaning, not obscured by the traditions of men.

Luke 19:10: "For the Son of Man came to seek and to save the lost." The question is this: Will Jesus Christ really do what He said He came here to do? He didn't say He came to save some of the lost. He came to save the lost. And that is everybody! Apart from Christ, we are all lost, but He came to seek for us until He finds us (Luke 15:4).

Luke 3:6: "All flesh shall see the salvation of God." This verse is probably taken from Isaiah 40:5, which says, "And the glory of the Lord shall be revealed, and all flesh shall see it together, for the mouth of the Lord has spoken." Surely these verses point in the direction of universal salvation. Matthew 5:8: "Blessed are the pure in heart, for they shall see God."

Luke 6:27–36:

> But I [Jesus] say to you who hear, Love your enemies, do good to those who hate you, bless those who curse you, pray for those who abuse you. To one who strikes you on the cheek, offer the other also, and from one who takes away your cloak do not withhold your tunic either. Give to everyone who begs from you, and from one who takes away your goods do not demand them back. And as you wish that others would do to you, do so to them.
>
> If you love those who love you, what benefit is that to you? For even sinners love those who love them. And if you do good to those who do good to

you, what benefit is that to you? For even sinners do the same. And if you lend to those from whom you expect to receive, what credit is that to you? Even sinners lend to sinners, to get back the same amount. But love your enemies, and do good, and lend, expecting nothing in return, and your reward will be great, and you will be sons of the Most High, for he is kind to the ungrateful and the evil. Be merciful, even as your Father is merciful.

If you are a Christian, you have probably read this passage many times to discover what kind of lifestyle Jesus expects from you. Have you ever thought of reading it as a description of God? Look at it in that light. Jesus says in the end that if you do these things, you will be like your Father, "for he is kind to the ungrateful and the evil" and "your Father is merciful." Remember also that He is unchanging. If God's attitude toward sinners now is love and mercy, it will always be. Could the loving God described above really be happy knowing that even one of His children created in His image is suffering unspeakable anguish in hell forever?

Matthew 12:29: "How can someone enter a strong man's house and plunder his goods, unless he first binds the strong man? Then indeed he may plunder his house." Luke 11:21–22: "When a strong man, fully armed, guards his own palace, his goods are safe; but when one stronger than he attacks him and overcomes him, he takes away his armor in which he trusted and divides his spoil." In these verses, the strong man is Satan, the stronger man is Christ, and the plunder or spoil is mankind. Jesus defeated Satan on the cross and He will eventually carry all of the spoils of that victory to be with Him. If anyone is eternally lost, Jesus' victory was only partial. In the NLT, Luke 11:22 is translated, "Until someone who is stronger attacks and overpowers him, strips him of his weapons, and carries off his belongings." Jesus won the right on the cross to strip Satan of all his belongings, and He will!

Luke 15:4: "What man of you, having a hundred sheep, if he has lost one of them, does not leave the ninety-nine in the open country, and go after the one that is lost, until he finds it?" Forgive me for coming back to this passage, but it is one of my favorites. To me it is so clear. If the average shepherd would keep on looking for one lost sheep and not give up until he finds it, surely our Lord will be no less persistent in seeking out every last one of His sheep, not just until they die, but until He finds them and brings them back safely to His fold. Praise His name forever! By asking, "What man of you…," Jesus gives clear sanction to the right to argue from those feelings shared even by the outcast and sinful, to the divine feelings as I have done in chapter 2. It is obvious that that is exactly what Jesus is doing here in this passage. It is as if He said, "If a shepherd won't give up until he finds one lost sheep, how much more will God refuse to give up on His children!"

John 1:6–7: "There was a man sent from God, whose name was John. He came as a witness, to bear witness about the light, that all might believe through him." That ALL might believe! That is God's stated reason for sending John, and that is His reason for all of His dealings with mankind. Dare we say that God will fail to accomplish His goal in sending John and all of the other prophets, and His only begotten Son?

John 1:29: "The next day he [John] saw Jesus coming toward him, and said, 'Behold, the Lamb of God, who is going to try to take away the sin of the world!'" Is that what it says? No! Jesus is "the Lamb of God, who takes away the sin of the world!" The sin of the whole world, not just a part of it. Will He do it? Does He work "all things according to the counsel of his will?" (Ephesians 1:11).

John 3:17: "God did not send his son into the world to condemn the world, but in order that the world might be saved through him." Again, why would God, who is all knowing, send Jesus to save the world if He knew beforehand that most of the world would not be saved? That doesn't make sense. God sent Jesus to save the world because He knew His Son would accomplish exactly what He sent Him to do.

John 3:35, 6:37–39: "The Father loves the Son and has given all things into his hand. All that the Father gives me will come to me, and whoever comes to me I will never cast out. For I have come from heaven, not to do my own will but the will of him who sent me. And this is the will of him who sent me, that I should lose nothing of all that he has given me, but raise it up on the last day." The false belief that salvation must take place before physical death necessitates explaining away even the clearest scriptures. If you believe that punishment after death is temporary and remedial, as I hope to show when we get to our study of the Greek words translated "eternal" and "everlasting," the above verses are crystal clear. The Father has promised the Son that everyone will eventually come to Him. He has given them to Him. Their destiny as redeemed children of God is sure!

John 6:33: "For the bread of God is he who comes down from heaven and gives life to the world." Notice He doesn't offer life to the world—He gives it! I am not saying faith and repentance are unnecessary. I am saying that verses like Philippians 2:10 about every knee bowing and every tongue confessing that Jesus Christ is Lord to the glory of God look forward to a time when everyone who has ever been born has come to faith and repentance.

John 12:32: "And I, when I am lifted up from the earth, will draw all people to myself." We have already looked at this verse. Remember Jesus didn't say that He would draw a select group called "The Elect"! He doesn't say He will try to draw all people to Himself. He says He will do it! He says in the words of a poet:

> So shall I lift up in My pierced hands
> Beyond the reach of grief and guilt
> The whole creation.
> —E.B. Browning

Matthew 11:27: "All things have been handed over to me by my Father, and no one knows the Son except the Father, and no one knows the Father except the Son and ANYONE to whom the Son chooses to reveal him." This verse says as clearly as it possibly can that the only thing necessary for anyone to know God is for Jesus to choose to reveal Him to them. Why would Jesus choose not to reveal the Father to anyone for whom He died?

In what has become known as the High Priestly Prayer, just before His betrayal and arrest, Jesus says in John 17:1–3: "Father, the hour has come; glorify your Son that the Son may glorify you, since you have given him authority over ALL flesh, to give eternal life to ALL whom you have given him. And this is eternal life, that they know you the only true God, and Jesus Christ whom you have sent." Who has the Father given to Jesus? All flesh. Or as John 3:35 says, "all things," or as John 12:32 says, "all people," the salvation of every person has been predestined from before the foundation of the world. The Father has given ALL mankind to Jesus, and He will draw them ALL to Himself in His time.

John 19:30: "When Jesus had received the sour wine, he said, 'It is finished.'" J.C. Ryle writes, "Our Lord meant that His great work of redemption was finished. He had as Daniel foretold, 'finished transgression, made an end of sin, made reconciliation for iniquity, and brought in everlasting righteousness' (Daniel 9:24). After thirty-three years, since the day when He was born in Bethlehem, He had done all, paid all, performed all, suffered all that was needful to save sinners and satisfy the justice of God. He had fought the battle and won it, and in two days He would give proof of it by rising again."

If the salvation of all men was not secured on the cross but only made available, it would have been far from finished. The battle would have just begun. The hard part would have been getting people to receive the salvation made available to them. People do need to receive it, but Jesus died knowing that they all eventually will because the Father had given them all to Him. It is finished! 1 John 2:2: "He is the propitiation for our sins, and not for ours only but also for the sins of the whole world."

So much for limited atonement! Jesus made atonement for the sins of the whole world. Would He who knows all things, who knows the beginning from the end, die for anyone unless He knew His death would have the desired effect of reconciling all people to God?

1 John 3:5: "You know that he [Jesus] appeared to take away sins, and in him there is no sin." Did Jesus really come just to take sin to hell and leave it there like a toxic waste dump, or did He come to annihilate it? Our next verse answers that question.

1 John 3:8: "The reason the Son of God appeared was to destroy the works of the devil." What is sin? The works of the devil. Jesus

came not to keep sin in hell forever but to destroy it. That is why 2 Peter 3:13 says, "But according to his promise we are waiting for new heavens and a new earth in which righteousness dwells." Some day the entire universe will be completely devoid of sin, and God will be all in all! There won't be a place called hell that is full of sin forever, because according to Revelation 20:14, "Death and Hades were thrown into the lake of fire," presumably for destruction.

1 John 4:14: "And we have seen and testify that the Father has sent his Son to be the Savior of the few who receive him in life, and to throw the rest into everlasting torment." Is that what it says? No, it says, "The Father has sent his Son to be the Savior of the world." Will He succeed, or will He fail?

Revelation 1:18: "I [Jesus] have the keys of Death and Hades." How can death eternally separate anyone from Christ when He has the keys of Death and Hades and He is not willing that any should perish, but that all should come to repentance?

Revelation 5:13: "And I [John] heard EVERY creature in heaven and on earth and under the earth and in the sea, and ALL that is in them, saying, 'To him who sits on the throne and to the Lamb be blessing and honor and glory and might forever and ever!'" How can people be left in hell weeping and wailing and gnashing their teeth if they are ALL gathered before the throne of God and the Lamb, worshipping them and ascribing to them blessing and honor and glory?

Ephesians 1:9–10: God's "purpose, which he set forth in Christ as a plan for the fullness of time," is to "unite ALL things in him [Christ], things in heaven and things on earth." What other meaning could these verses possibly have than the clear meaning that is right there? In the fullness of time, ALL things ("all people," according to the context) will be united in Christ and God will be all in all! That is why Paul talks in verse 12 about "we who were the first to hope in Christ." We who are believers now are the firstfruits. The rest will follow in due time.

Acts 3:21 (NLT): Jesus "must remain in heaven until the time for the final restoration of ALL things, as God promised long ago through the prophets." Again, what else could this refer to but the complete restoration of every child of God created in His image to a right relationship with Him?

Acts 24:14–15: "I [Paul] worship the God of our fathers, believing everything laid down by the Law and written in the Prophets, having a hope in God ... that there will be a resurrection of both the just and the unjust." This is the same man who said in Romans 9:3: "I could wish that I myself were accursed and cut off from Christ for the sake of my brothers." Would he hope for the resurrection of the unjust knowing that they were being raised only to be thrown body and soul into a place of torment forever?

We have been looking mostly at the Gospels and Acts. Now we turn to the letters of Paul. We will find in them the stream of promise still widening, the universal nature of redemption indicated with a precision of language and a variety of illustrations that seem impossible to reconcile with endless evil. I don't mean that every passage quoted is in itself conclusive. I do mean that all are relevant, as links in the great chain of promise, which taken together make a very strong case for universal restoration, which brings up an important question: If we are to believe in endless evil and endless suffering, how can we account for such passages that, taken in their natural meaning, obviously point to the wider hope?

That the Bible holds out the hope of universal restoration and reconciliation cannot be denied (Acts 3:21; Colossians 1:20). If this will never take place, why is it in the Bible? Why does the Bible raise expectations that will never be fulfilled?

Paul's writings deserve special notice. His writings are the closest thing to a systematic theology in the Bible ranging over the whole field of the divine purpose and human destiny. I want to draw your attention to two points:

1. Not only does Paul assert the sovereignty of God, but it also lies at the center of his teaching. He sees everywhere a purpose slowly but surely fulfilling itself, a purpose that can be resisted but not defeated.
2. He gives striking prominence to the resurrection as a spiritual and redemptive force. It is the climax of Christ's work for man.

In Romans 4:13, he says that God promised "Abraham and his offspring that he would be heir of the world." God chose Abraham not for Abraham's sake only, but also that he might inherit the world. This is a spiritual inheritance, not physical. In verse 17, Paul cites Genesis 17:5: "As it is written, 'I have made you the father of many nations.'"

Romans 5:18: "Therefore, as one trespass led to condemnation for ALL men, so one act of righteousness leads to justification and life for ALL men." This passage couldn't be more explicit. Everyone who was condemned by Adam's sin will be justified by Christ's death. If the word "ALL" means "all mankind" in the first part of the verse, it means "all mankind" in the second part. I highly recommend studying the entire passage (Romans 5:12–21) without a commentary. Commentators will just try to explain away the clear teaching of this passage, which is that grace is always stronger than sin.

Romans 5:15: "If many [everyone] died through one man's [Adam's] trespass, much more have the grace of God and the free gift [salvation] by the grace of that one man Jesus Christ abounded for many [everyone]." This verse is another example of those who believe in eternal hell changing the meaning of a word in the same sentence. In the first part of the verse, they say the word "many" refers to all men because Adam's trespass brought death on all mankind, but when Paul uses the same word in the second half of the same sentence, they say it refers only to those who are born again before they die, because they refuse to believe that God's grace will reach every man. Paul clearly says in this verse that the grace of God and the free gift of salvation abounds for everyone!

Romans 11:11–31:

> So I ask, did they [Israel] stumble in order that they might fall? By no means! Rather through their trespass salvation has come to the Gentiles, so as to make Israel jealous. Now if their trespass means riches for the world, and if their failure means riches for the Gentiles, how much more will their full inclusion mean!
>
> Now I am speaking to you Gentiles. Inasmuch

then as I am an apostle to the Gentiles, I magnify my ministry in order somehow to make my fellow Jews jealous, and thus save some of them. For if their rejection means the reconciliation of the world, what will their acceptance mean but life from the dead? If the dough offered as firstfruits is holy, so is the whole lump, and if the root is holy, so are the branches.

But if some of the branches were broken off, and you, although a wild olive shoot, were grafted in among the others and now share in the nourishing root of the olive tree, do not be arrogant toward the branches. If you are, remember it is not you who support the root, but the root that supports you. Then you will say, "Branches were broken off so that I might be grafted in." That is true. They were broken off because of their unbelief, but you stand fast through faith. So do not become proud, but stand in awe. For if God did not spare the natural branches, neither will he spare you. Note then the kindness and the severity of God: severity toward those who have fallen, but God's kindness to you, provided you continue in his kindness. Otherwise you too will be cut off. And even they, if they do not continue in their unbelief, will be grafted in, for God has the power to graft them in again. For if you were cut from what is by nature a wild olive tree, and grafted, contrary to nature, into a cultivated olive tree, how much more will these, the natural branches, be grafted back into their own olive tree.

Lest you be wise in your own conceits, I want you to understand this mystery, brothers: a partial hardening has come upon Israel, until the fullness of the Gentiles has come in. And in this way all Israel will be saved, as it is written, "The Deliverer will come from Zion, he will banish ungodliness from Jacob; and this will be my covenant with them when I take away their sins." As regards the gospel, they are enemies of God for your sake. But as regards election, they are beloved for the sake of their forefathers. For the gifts and the calling of God are irrevocable. Just as you were at one time disobedient to God but now have received mercy because of their disobedience, so they too have now been disobedient in order that by the mercy shown to you they also may now receive mercy.

Study this passage carefully and prayerfully and see how God, the Master Strategist, is working everything together toward a goal that cannot fail! What is that goal? The next verse tells us. Romans 11:32: "For God has consigned ALL to disobedience, that he may have mercy on ALL." God chooses this person or nation and hardens that person or nation not to save a select group called "the elect" as Calvinists would have us believe, but so that "he may have mercy on all."

Romans 11:36: "For from him and through him and to him are all things. To him be glory forever. Amen." Look at each part of this declaration one at a time. "For from him ... are all things." This obviously means that all things have their origin in Him. He created every thing. "Through him ... are all things" Everything is sustained by Him. "To him are all things." As all things had their origin in Him, so they will return to Him. To Him be glory forever!! Amen!

Romans 14:11: "As I live, says the Lord, every knee shall bow to me, and every tongue shall confess to God." The margin of the ESV says, "Or shall give praise." The NASB translates it: "Every tongue shall give praise to God." The CEV: "Everyone will kneel down and praise my name!" The words are self-explanatory. Everyone will praise God!

1 Corinthians 15:22: "As in Adam ALL die, so also in Christ shall ALL be made alive." *The Message* translates it: "Everybody dies in Adam; everybody comes alive in Christ." Again I would ask you, Does it really make sense to take the first "all" to mean everyone and confine the second "all" to those who die in Christ? It is obvious that Paul has the same group in mind in both halves of the verse.

1 Corinthians 15:22–28:

> For as in Adam all die, so also in Christ shall all be made alive. But each in his own order: Christ the firstfruits, then at his coming those who belong to Christ. Then comes the end, when he delivers the kingdom to God the Father after destroying every rule and every authority and power. For he must reign until he has put all his enemies under his feet. The last enemy to be destroyed is death. For "God has put all things in subjection under his feet." But when it says, "all things are put in subjection," it is plain that he is excepted who put all things in subjection under him. When all things are subjected to him, then the Son himself will also be subjected to him who put all things in subjection under him, that God may be all in all.

At the end, there is no place for sin, evil, or hell, for God is all in all!

If God has to cast some people into everlasting hell, it means that He was unable to get them to submit themselves to Him. They won't be submitting themselves to Him in hell; they will be hating Him and cursing Him for all eternity. What kind of subjection is that? All will willingly subject themselves to Jesus and to God the Father after He has purged them of all sin and rebellion. The same word is used of Christ's subjection to the Father, and of the subjection of Christ's enemies to Him. Obviously Christ's subjection to the Father is out of love. How can endless evil and torment be described as subjection to Jesus? Such an interpretation is excluded by the last statement in this passage: "that God may be all in all"!

1 Corinthians 15:55: "O death, where is your victory? O death, where is your sting?" If the majority of mankind will go to everlasting hell after death, it would seem that death will have won a gigantic victory! I urge you to study this entire section of scripture (1 Corinthians 15:12–58) and notice Paul's increasing rapture as his argument expands, as the prospect opens up to him of a universe yet to be, from which all sin and death are wiped out. Paul's words give only an imperfect expression of the absolute triumph of Christ, of

the flood of glory that will fill the universe in the widest possible sense. God will be all in all!

2 Corinthians 5:19: "In Christ God was reconciling the world to himself." Note that it doesn't say God was trying to reconcile the world to Himself. He was doing it! Study this whole passage carefully (2 Corinthians 5:11–21). God's reconciliation of the world to Himself is an accomplished fact. When we tell others about Christ, we are just telling them to embrace what has already been accomplished. And if they don't do it in this life, they will in the life to come when EVERY knee shall bow and EVERY tongue shall confess that Jesus Christ is Lord to the glory of God!

Ephesians 1:9–10: "His purpose, which he set forth in Christ as a plan for the fullness of time," is "to unite ALL things in him, things in heaven and things on earth." If all things in heaven and earth are to be united in Christ, how is there any possibility of an endless hell or a creation permanently divided?

Ephesians 1:22–23: "And he [the Father] put all things under his [Jesus'] feet and gave him as head over all things to the church, which is his body, the fullness of him who fills all in all." The Greek verb used here for all things being under Christ's feet is used in 1 Corinthians 15:28, referring to the subjection of Christ to the Father. As we saw in looking at that verse, Christ's subjection of Himself to the Father is willing submission out of His love for the Father. That is the same submission Jesus will someday have from "all things." Notice the last phrase of verse 23: "the fullness of him who fills all in all." God fills everything in every way. The idea of a place existing for all eternity where people are forever shut out from the presence of God doesn't fit in a universe where God fills all in all.

Ephesians 4:8: "When he ascended on high he led a host of captives, and he gave gifts to men." Who are these captives? Luke 11:22, which we have already looked at, tells us. When Christ, the stronger man, broke into the strong man's (Satan's) house, he carried away all his belongings. 1 Peter 3:19, 4:6 tells us that Christ went and proclaimed the gospel to the spirits in prison (Hades) that they might live in the Spirit as God does.

Ephesians 4:10: "He who descended is the one who ascended far above all the heavens, that he might fill all things." As we saw in looking at Ephesians 1:23, if Christ fills all things, how can there be an everlasting hell where people are forever shut out from the presence of Christ? The doctrine of eternal hell totally contradicts so many verses of scripture. The day is coming when God will completely eradicate sin from existence, not just keep it tucked away in a dark corner of the universe called hell forever!

Colossians 1:19–20: Through Christ "God was pleased ... to reconcile to himself ALL things, whether on earth or in heaven, making peace by the blood of his cross." If God's goal in sending Christ was to reconcile everything to Himself, nothing can thwart that goal because He "works all things according to the counsel of his will" (Ephesians 1:11).

Philippians 2:10–11: "At the name of Jesus every knee should bow, in heaven and on earth and under the earth, and every tongue confess that Jesus Christ is Lord, to the glory of God the Father." Don't let that word "should" throw you. The NASB, NLT, NCV, CEV, *The Message,* and other translations all say "will." The key phrase is "to the glory of God ."

If people are just bowing outwardly out of fear or awe while their hearts remain unbowed, that doesn't glorify God. Some day, every creature everywhere will willingly bow in worship and adoration as it says so clearly in our next verse, Revelation 5:13: "And I heard every creature in heaven and on earth and under the earth and in the sea, and all that is in them, saying, 'To him who sits on the throne and to the Lamb be blessing and honor and glory and might forever and ever!'" This is so obviously genuine worship! Would God who loves all mankind really cast anyone into everlasting torment who worships Him like this? Obviously John is looking past the judgment to a time when everyone everywhere has at last been reconciled to God and God is all in all! Hallelujah!!

In my church we sing a song called "Ancient of Days," which quotes this verse almost verbatim. It goes, "Blessing and honor, glory and power be unto Him who sits on the throne. From every nation all of creation bows before the Ancient of Days. Every tongue in heaven and earth shall declare your glory. Every knee shall bow at your throne in worship." Too bad I seem to be the only one in my church who believes the words as they're being sung.

Philippians 3:20–21: "But our citizenship is in heaven, and from it we await a Savior, the Lord Jesus Christ, who will transform our lowly body to be like his glorious body, by the power that enables him to subject all things to himself." The way that the subjection of all things to Christ is to be understood is clear from the context, "who will transform our body to be like his glorious body." No believer doubts that Christ is able to subdue all things to Himself, but this passage shows decisively what that means. It is making them like Himself, not casting them into everlasting torment!

1 Timothy 2:3–6: "This is good, and it is pleasing in the sight of God our Savior, who desires all people to be saved and to come to the knowledge of the truth. For there is one God, and there is one mediator between God and men, the man Christ Jesus, who gave himself as a ransom for all, which is the testimony given at the proper time." There are basically three ways this passage can be interpreted:

1. The Arminian—God desires all people to be saved. He gave His only Begotten Son to save everyone. But He can't save anyone except those who are willing to be saved.
2. The Calvinist—God has two wills that "appear" to contradict each other—His revealed will and His secret will. Even though His expressed will is for all people to be saved, He really doesn't want anyone to be saved except for the elect whom He chose before the foundation of the world, and whom He effectually calls to Himself. They call this "apparent" contradiction a paradox or an antinomy. But if it walks like a duck and quacks like a duck, it's probably a duck. In other words, if it looks like a contradiction and sounds like a contradiction, it probably is.
3. The Universalist—God wants all men to be saved. He sent Jesus to die for all men. God is sovereign. Therefore all will eventually be saved.

Unfortunately these are not straw men. I have heard and read each of these views from those who hold them. Which one sounds most plausible?

1 Timothy 4:10: "We have our hope set on the living God, who is the Savior of all people, especially of those who believe." The meaning is so clear it's transparent! God IS the Savior of everyone! He is the Savior of believers now and He will save everyone else in due time.

2 Timothy 1:10: "Our Savior Christ Jesus ... abolished death and brought life and immortality to light through the gospel." Jesus has abolished death, and with death what it implies in scripture—sin and evil. Death abolished and death in its worst form, the second death, maintained forever, are plain contradictions.

Titus 2:11: "For the grace of God has appeared, bringing salvation for all people." How is God's grace bringing salvation for all people consistent with the eternal damnation of anyone?

1 Peter 3:19: Christ "went and proclaimed to the spirits in prison." 1 Peter 4:6 tells us what was preached to them. Was it their eternal damnation? No, it was the Gospel. It says, "The gospel was preached even to those who are dead, that though judged in the flesh the way people are, they might live in the spirit the way God does.

J.C. Ryle says, "Some theologians hold that, between His death and resurrection 'He went and preached to the spirits in prison' (1 Peter 3:19) and proclaimed the accomplishment of His work of atonement." Although he himself considered this "doubtful," he says this view was held by Athanasius, Ambrose, Zwingle, Calvin, Erasmus, Calovius, and Alford. This is the most natural way to interpret these verses if you don't have to try to prove the unbiblical teaching that all chance for salvation ends at death.

2 Peter 3:9: "The Lord is ... not wishing that any should perish, but that all should reach repentance." The NIV translates it: "The Lord is ... not wanting anyone to perish." If the Lord does not want anyone to perish, we can rest assured no one will. We have already shown in chapter 2 that God is able to change people's hearts and make them willing to come to Him even if they come "kicking, struggling, and resentful" as C.S. Lewis so eloquently put it in his testimony.

Hebrews 1:2: "He [God] has spoken to us by his Son, whom he appointed the heir of all things." What sort of things do you suppose Jesus Christ is interested in inheriting? Mankind!

Psalm 2:7–8: "The Lord said to me, 'You are my Son; today I have begotten you. Ask of me, and I will make the nations your heritage, and the ends of the earth your possession.'" This verse is used in missions textbooks all the time. God has promised to give His Son all the nations as His inheritance, and He will do it!

Hebrews 2:5–9:

> Now it was not to angels that God subjected the world to come, of which we are speaking. It has been testified somewhere, "What is man, that you are mindful of him, or the son of man, that you care for him? You made him for a little while lower than the angels; you have crowned him with glory and honor, putting everything in subjection under his feet." Now in putting everything in subjection to him, he left NOTHING outside his control. At present, we do not yet see everything in subjection to him. But we see him who for a little while was made lower than the angels, namely Jesus, crowned with glory and honor because of the suffering of death, so that by the grace of God he might taste death for EVERYONE.

Here is one more passage to add to the many that speak of Christ's kingdom being destined to extend over all things. I have already shown that subjection to Christ means not the subjugation of slaves, but perfect harmony and peace in the New Testament. The subjection of mankind will be like Christ's subjection to the Father, done out of love. (See notes on Philippians 3:21 and 1 Corinthians 15:25.) Christ has tasted death for everyone! Therefore all will be saved in due time.

Hebrews 2:14–15: "Since therefore the children share in flesh and blood, he himself likewise partook of the same things, that through death he might destroy the one who has the power of death, that is, the devil, and deliver ALL those who through fear of death were subject to lifelong slavery." If Jesus' death destroyed the devil as to his having the power of death, how can death continue forever in hell? If Christ's death delivers ALL from the fear of death, how can eternal death be waiting for anyone?

Hebrews 6:17 (NIV): "Because God wanted to make the unchanging nature of his purpose very clear to the heirs of what was promised, he confirmed it with an oath." We see God's unchanging purpose clearly in 2 Peter 3:9 where it says that God is not willing for anyone to perish. The word translated "willing" there is a variant of the word translated "purpose" in Hebrews 6:17.

If God's purpose or will is unchanging, and He is not willing that any should perish, we can be sure that God's purpose will come to pass in His time!

Hebrews 9:26: "He [Jesus] has appeared once for all at the end of the ages to put away sin by the sacrifice of himself." The NIV translates it, "To do away with sin." That is the question: Did Jesus come to completely do away with sin or just to safely contain it in hell forever? If sin exists forever, Christ's victory is incomplete, because He came to do away with it completely! Amen!

Hebrews 13:8: "Jesus Christ is the same yesterday and today and forever." The same Lord Jesus Christ that loved sinners when He was here in the flesh, who prayed for those who nailed Him to the cross, "Father, forgive them, for they know not what they do," that same Jesus will love sinners forever because He is unchanging!

A few words of caution must be added here. I hope I have made it clear that in teaching universal salvation, I have not tried to minimize sin, nor have I taught that sinners will be saved while still clinging to their sins. I believe that many people have terrible sufferings awaiting them after they leave this life—how long and how severe I leave up to a loving and just God. But I believe that God never punishes for punishment's sake. He always has the sinner's repentance and restoration in view, and in His wisdom He knows exactly what it will take in each case to bring about the desired results!

I am opposed to the popular creed partially because I believe that it in fact teaches men to make light of sin in two ways: first, because it teaches a plan of retribution that is so unjust as to make people secretly believe its penalties will never be inflicted; and next, because it asserts that God either will not, or cannot, overcome and destroy evil and sin, but will bear with them for ever and ever. I repeat that not a single word has been written in these pages that would indicate that God is just a "good ol' boy" who winks at sin and considers it a light matter when someone violates His holy law! God forbid that I should teach such shallow theology! It is in the light of Golgotha that we see sin as exceedingly sinful, so sinful that nothing less than the death of God incarnate could pay for it. But let us be careful, lest in thinking we are honoring the atonement we are actually dishonoring it by limiting its power to save by teaching that Christ failed in His mission as Savior of the world, making Him a liar. Because He never said, "If I am lifted up I will draw SOME men to myself," or "I will TRY to draw all men to myself," but, "I WILL draw ALL MEN to myself!"

CHAPTER 12

What the New Testament Teaches, Continued

He has appeared once for all at the end of the ages to put away sin by the sacrifice of himself. (Hebrews 9:26)

Universalists are sometimes accused of focusing on God's love to the exclusion of His justice and holiness. I am determined that in these pages there will be no room left for such a charge. I firmly believe that it is those who would make such a charge who have a perverted view of God's love and justice. It is very true that there is a current that runs through Holy Scripture that seems to the English-speaking reader to teach either the destruction or eternal punishment of those who die apart from Christ. I fully admit this. The key word here is "seems." The Bible was not written in English but in Hebrew, Aramaic, and Greek. It comes to us from very distant ages, in very many parts, the work of about forty different inspired authors, all of them writing from an Eastern standpoint, saturated with Eastern habits of thought, and with Eastern phrases and style. Therefore, true interpretation of Scripture depends to a great degree on understanding the sense in which the terms in question are used. Let us go to the Bible with this in mind.

Admitting that there runs through Scripture these two currents of God's love for all men and the awful punishment waiting for those who die in their sins, we feel instinctively that love and not wrath is the central theme of God's revelation to us. We feel its kinship with all that is noblest in our nature. I don't just mean with what we like better, but with what we recognize as best and most divine both in God and in mankind. Some may say that the current of wrath is louder, but I don't think so. It may seem so to some from habit, or because sinners do not readily grasp what is broadest and most divine. To them, revenge is more credible than mercy and love. Even if wrath were the louder current, I would point out that God is usually heard in a still, small voice.

That which seems to be the meaning of a passage of Scripture on the surface may not necessarily be the true meaning. The Israelites didn't recognize Jesus as their Messiah because they read the prophecies concerning His second coming in power and glory and applied them to His first coming when He came as a suffering servant. The truth was under the surface in those fewer, less prominent predictions of the latter, but they couldn't see it because they wanted a conquering King to throw off the yoke of their Roman oppressors. I want to honestly face all the facts, and I urge you to try to open your mind to the possibility that you may have missed the truth of God's love, which (as 1 Corinthians 13 tells us) never fails because of a false understanding of God's justice and wrath. I hope to show that while the penalties threatened against sinners are truly terrible, still they are not endless. I believe that not one passage found anywhere in the Bible teaches endless suffering when fairly translated and understood. I ask you before examining these passages to keep several things in mind:

1. When the horrors of endless sin and pain are so staunchly defended on the (supposed) authority of the Bible, it is well to remember that slavery was almost unanimously defended for hundreds of years on similar grounds, as were the infliction of cruel tortures, religious persecution with its indescribable horrors, and the burning of witches. During the dark ages, theologians actually believed that demons had sexual intercourse with humans. You may say, "All the leading Bible teachers defend eternal hell on the authority of

Scripture." I would reply, "Bible teachers have defended doctrines and practices so abominable that one can hardly imagine anyone believing such things, much less ministers of the Gospel of Jesus Christ!

2. This is a fact of the deepest significance: Although certain words and phrases existed that Jesus and the Apostles could have used to convey the concept of unendingness, they never used these words in regard to the future punishment of unrepentant sinners! This will be shown as we progress.

3. Thus *aiidios* or *ateleutetos* are never used of future punishment in the New Testament. Nor is it ever said to be *aneutelous,* "without end." Nor do we read that it shall go on *pantote* or *eis to dienekes,* "forever."

4. Is it, I ask, conceivable that a sentence so awful as to be absolutely beyond all human thought should be pronounced against millions of hapless creatures in ambiguous language that is clearly capable of another meaning, and often clearly used in the New Testament and in the Greek translation of the Old Testament (which our Lord and His Apostles quote from) to convey that other meaning?

5. If Jesus really taught everlasting punishment, why is it that the book of Acts, which records many of the first Christian sermons ever preached, does not contain a single word about hell? If Jesus had really taught His disciples that everlasting torment awaited anyone who rejected their message, would they not have warned people about it?

6. It is surely a strong confirmation of universal salvation that many of the earliest Christian theologians who spoke Greek fluently did not understand the words *aion* or *ainios* to mean "everlasting" but taught rather that all would eventually be reconciled to God. All such teaching obviously implies that the texts usually relied on do not teach eternal punishment.

7. The texts quoted in favor of universal salvation use clear, explicit language and are a fair translation of the original in every case. This cannot be said with regard to the passages usually alleged to teach endless torment. In every verse that

seems to the English-speaking reader to teach everlasting hell, they are either mistranslated, misinterpreted, or both. Thus we see how inaccurate the assumption is that is so widely made that these terms that seem to teach endless pain and evil are in the Bible. They are merely in fallible translations of the Bible, which is a totally different thing.

8. It should be noted that not a few of the passages usually quoted in support of the traditional creed teach not the eternal torment but the destruction of the wicked, which Universalists understand to mean the destruction of the sinful nature.

9. Finally, in addition to all the above, a huge obstacle remains in the way of the advocates of the traditional creed, which is this: They don't carry out their own principles. Their principles of interpreting the Bible would compel them to believe and to teach what no reasonable person would presume to teach. First, it would compel them to believe in the endless torment of the vast majority, at least of all adults. Next, it would compel them to believe that this torment goes on forever and ever in the sight of the Lamb and the holy angels. Revelation 14:10–11 says that anyone who worships the beast "will drink the wine of God's wrath, poured full strength into the cup of his anger, and he will be tormented with fire and sulfur in the presence of the holy angels and in the presence of the Lamb. And the smoke of their torment goes up forever and ever, and they have no rest, day or night, these worshipers of the beast and its image, and whoever receives the mark of its name." The words translated "forever and ever" should be translated "for ages and ages." That is terrifying enough without making it forever! The advocates of eternal hell believe that the saints will also be watching the eternal suffering of the damned. Luke 16:23: "And in Hades, being in torment, he lifted up his eyes and saw Abraham far off and Lazarus at his side." Some have even said that the saints will enjoy seeing the suffering of the damned. As I said before, may God deliver me from ever being that cruel!

10. As instances of incorrect translations, take the words translated "hell," "damnation," "everlasting," "eternal," "forever and ever." In the New Testament, "hell" is a translation of three widely different Greek words: "Hades," "Gehenna," and "Tarturus." "Gehenna" occurs eleven times in the New Testament as used by our Lord and once by James. In the original Greek, it is taken almost unchanged from the Hebrew (Ge-hinnom, i.e., valley of Hinnom), an example that our translators should have followed and rendered it "Gehenna" as it is. By translating it to the word "hell" with all of its connotations, they are assuming the part of commentators instead of translators.

The valley of Hinnom lay outside of Jerusalem. Once a pleasant valley, it later became the scene of Molech worship. 2 Kings 23:10 tells how the reformer king Josiah put a stop to people burning their sons and daughters there as offerings to Molech, a pagan god. 2 Chronicles 28:3 tells how evil king Ahaz "made offerings in the Valley of the Son of Hinnom and burned his sons as an offering, according to the abominations of the nations whom the Lord drove out before the people of Israel." In 2 Chronicles 33:6, King Manasseh of Judah "burned his sons as an offering in the Valley of the Son of Hinnom, and used fortune-telling and omens and sorcery, and dealt with mediums and with wizards. He did much evil in the sight of the Lord, provoking Him to anger." In Jeremiah 32:35, God says of both Judah and Israel, "They built the high places of Baal in the Valley of the Son of Hinnom, to offer up their sons and daughters to Molech, though I did not command them, nor did it enter my mind, that they should do this abomination, to cause Judah to sin." The Valley of Hinnom later became a garbage dump. Into it all sorts of waste and carcasses were thrown and a fire was kept burning all the time while the worms ate what was left.

The next term is "Hades." This is used to denote the state or place of spirits, both good and bad alike, after death, and it has nothing to do with punishment. It occurs five times in the Gospels and Epistles, twice in Acts, and four times in Revelation.

"Tartarus" occurs only once in the New Testament in 2 Peter 2:4: "God did not spare angels when they sinned, but cast them into hell and committed them to chains of gloomy darkness to be kept until the judgment." Here Peter applies this term not to human beings but to fallen angels, and even they are not kept there forever, but while they are awaiting the judgment. Hence to render it as "hell" is preposterous.

"Damnation" and "damned" are both translations of the Greek words *krino* and *katarino,* meaning "to judge" or "to condemn." Neither word contains the idea of everlasting torment. The English word "damn" carries with it the connotation of everlasting hell. But the Greek word merely means to judge, which by no means carries that terrifying connotation.

The word "hell" simply means the place of disembodied spirits when it translates as "Hades," or when the word "Gehenna" is used, it is a reference to the valley of Hinnom, where the worms fed continually on the filth that was dumped into it and the fire was kept burning not to inflict torment but to purify. Bodies thrown there felt no pain from the worms or the fire be cause they were already dead. It is true that "Gehenna" was used symbolically of the place of future punishment. But there is nothing inherent in the word that denotes everlasting torment.

While I believe our Lord did not threaten everlasting torment if His words are correctly understood, yet they do convey a solemn warning to sinners. This warning should hold more weight than threats of eternal torment because the conscience can see the justice in it. I accept every warning, however terrible, and every penalty threatened against sinners as long as they are understood in what I believe to be their natural sense, which is not, as I hope to show, everlasting torment.

At last we come to one of the most important parts of our study.

Do the Greek words translated "eternal," "everlasting," "forever," and "forever and ever" really mean any of those things or not? The words in question are *aion* and *aionios*. I hope to show that the answer is a definite no!

The doctrine of eternal torment hinges on a mistranslation of these words. I hope to show what they mean—an age or an indefinite period of time varying in duration, depending on the subject being referred to. G. Campbell Morgan, a well-known Bible expositor of the twentieth century who was an associate of D.L. Moody and the pastor of Westminster Chapel where Dr. D. Martyn Lloyd Jones served as his associate pastor, wrote in his book *God's Methods with Men* (pages 185–186): "Let me say to Bible students that we must be very careful how we use the word 'eternity.' We have fallen into grave error in our constant use of that word. There is no word in the whole book of God corresponding with our 'eternal,' which as commonly used among us means absolutely without end. The strongest Scripture word used with reference to the existence of God is 'unto the ages of the ages,' which does not literally mean eternally."

In fact, even the English word "eternal" did not originally mean "having no end." *The Concise Dictionary of English Etymology*, first published in 1882 by Walter Skeat, says that the word "eternal" comes from the Latin *aternus*, which means, literally, "lasting for an age."

There are many things in the old covenant that are said to be everlasting, eternal, forever and ever that clearly are not. Some of them were types and shadows pointing to Christ. Alexander Cruden writes in his *Complete Concordance*, "Many believe that the words for ever or everlasting are not to be taken as synonymous with eternal, as being without end, but to be understood merely as meaning a very long time, to be left indeterminate. There seems to be a considerable amount of argument in favor of this in many cases." An example of this is Abraham:

> Genesis 13:15: "For all the land that you see I will give to you and to your offspring forever."

Hebrews 11:8–10: "By faith Abraham obeyed when he was called to go out to a place that he was to receive as an inheritance. And he went out, not knowing where he was going. By faith he went to live in the land of promise, as in a foreign land, living in tents with Isaac and Jacob, heirs with him of the same promise. For he was looking forward to the city that has foundations, whose designer and builder is God."

Hebrews 11:13–16 says of Abraham and the other heroes of the faith spoken of in this chapter, "These all died in faith, not having received the things promised, but having seen them and greeted them from afar, and having acknowledged that they were strangers and exiles on the earth. For people who speak thus make it clear that they are seeking a homeland. If they had been thinking of that land from which they had gone out, they would have had opportunity to return. But as it is, they desire a better country, that is, a heavenly one. Therefore God is not ashamed to be called their God, for he has prepared for them a city."

The truth is that Abraham's literal offspring have not lived in the promised land all the time since God promised it to Abraham, and they will not live there forever because this earth as we know it will not exist forever.

Exodus 12:14: "This day [Passover] shall be for you a memorial day, and you shall keep it as a feast to the Lord; throughout your generations, as a statute forever, you shall keep it as a feast." 1 Corinthians 5:7: "Christ, our Passover lamb, has been sacrificed." The Passover, which was supposed to be kept forever, was superseded by Christ, our Passover lamb.

Exodus 21:5–6: "But if the slave plainly says, 'I love my master, my wife, and my children; I will not go out free,' then his master shall bring him to God, and he shall bring him to the door or the doorpost. And his master shall bore his ear through with an awl, and he shall be his slave forever." I ask you, does this verse teach that there are people who will be slaves for all eternity?

Exodus 31:17: "It [the Sabbath] is a sign forever between me and the people of Israel." Colossians 2:16–17: "Therefore let no one pass judgment on you in questions of food and drink, or with regard to a festival or a new moon or a Sabbath. These are a shadow of the things to come, but the substance belongs to Christ." I could go on and on, giving quote after quote illustrating the fact that "forever" doesn't always mean forever, but I'm sure you get the picture.

The very existence of Christianity is proof of the temporary nature of things that are said in the Old Testament to be eternal or forever but have been superseded by Christ.

In the Septuagint, the Greek version of the Old Testament that was used by Our Lord and the Apostles, the words *aion* and *aionios* are repeatedly used of things that ceased to exist a long time ago.

Numbers 25:13 says of the Aaronic priesthood that it "shall be ... a perpetual priesthood." Deuteronomy 23:3: "No Ammonite or Moabite may enter the assembly of the Lord. Even to the tenth generation, none of them may enter the assembly of the Lord forever." Which is it? To the tenth generation or forever? It sounds as if both terms are used as figures of speech, meaning for a long, long time.

In talking about slaves, Leviticus 25:46 says, "You may bequeath them to your sons after you to inherit as a possession forever." I ask again, are they going to be slaves for all eternity?

Let us move on to the New Testament, where there are many instances where these words *aion* and *aionios* cannot possibly mean forever. My point is that if these words can and must be translated to mean a time of limited duration in many places where they are used in the New Testament, why would anyone want to translate them as "eternal" in the places they are used to speak of the punishment of those who die apart from a saving relationship with Christ?

The teachings of Scripture must be harmonized with each other as much as possible. If a teaching appears to contradict a clear teaching of Scripture, it is probably a false teaching. God's love for sinners and His desire for all mankind to be saved are arguably some of the clearest teachings in all of Scripture. These truths cannot possibly be harmonized with everlasting torment!

Let's look at some of the verses I spoke of where these words cannot mean "eternal," "eternity," "everlasting," or any such thing.

Matthew 12:32: "And whoever speaks a word against the Son of Man will be forgiven, but whoever speaks against the Holy Spirit will not be forgiven, either in this *aion* or in the one to come." If the word *aion* were translated "eternity" in this verse, it would obviously be teaching that there are at least two eternities, which is of course an absurdity because eternity is supposed to encompass all of time, even before time, and when time as we know it no longer exists.

Matthew 13:22: "As for what was sown among thorns, this is the one who hears the word, but the cares of the *aion* and the deceitfulness of riches choke the word, and it proves unfruitful." Do the cares of eternity choke the word and make it unfruitful? Of course not. Colossians 3:2 urges us to "set your minds on things that are above, not on things that are on earth."

Matthew 13:39: "The harvest is the close of the *aion,* and the reapers are angels." If *aion* were translated "eternity" here, it would of course teach the end of all things, even God, if God inhabits eternity and eternity comes to a close.

Luke 1:70: "As he spoke by the mouth of his holy prophets from of *aionos*." Have God's prophets been speaking forever?

In Luke 16:8, where Jesus tells the parable of the unjust steward or manager, He said, "The master commended the dishonest manager for his shrewdness. For the sons of this *aionios* are more shrewd in dealing with their own generation than the sons of light." Is this verse saying that the sons of this eternity are shrewder than the sons of light? Of course not!

Luke 18:29–30: "And he [Jesus] said to them [the twelve disciples], 'Truly I say to you, there is no one who has left house or wife or brothers or parents or children, for the sake of the kingdom of God, who will not receive many times more in this time, and in the *aioni* to come *aionion* life.'" Is Jesus saying, "In the eternity to come you will receive eternal life"? This doesn't make sense because there is not a present eternity and an eternity to come. There can only be one eternity.

Luke 20:34–35: "And Jesus said to them [the Sadducees], 'The sons of this *aionos* marry and are given in marriage, but those who are considered worthy to attain to that *aionos* and to the resurrection from the dead neither marry nor are given in marriage.'" If this word *aionos* was translated eternity, it would again be teaching that there are two eternities.

Apart from the verses about the destinies of the saved and the not yet saved, there are many, many more passages I could point out, but I'll cite just a few more.

Romans 12:2: "Do not be conformed to this *aioni,* but be transformed by the renewal of your mind." Does this verse teach us not to be conformed to eternity? Of course not! As in all of these passages, the meaning is clear: We are not to be conformed to this age.

1 Corinthians 1:20: "Where is the one who is wise? Where is the scribe? Where is the debater of this *aionos?* Has not God made foolish the wisdom of this world?" Is Paul asking, "Where is the debater of this eternity?" Obviously not.

Galatians 1:3–4: "Grace to you and peace from God our Father and the Lord Jesus Christ, who gave himself for our sins to deliver us from the present evil *aionos,* according to the will of our God and Father, to whom be the glory for *aionas* and *aionon.*" Did Jesus deliver us from this evil eternity, according to the will of God, to whom be glory for eternity and eternity? This is the kind of absurdity that translating these words as eternal, everlasting, etc., leads to. The meaning of these words is clearly "age." The only reason they were ever translated as "everlasting" was to try to prove the blasphemous doctrine of everlasting torment that was invented by the Roman Catholic Church to try to scare people into the Kingdom of God!

Let me state the dilemma clearly. *Aion* means either "forever" as its necessary, or at least its usual significance, or it doesn't. If it does, the following difficulties arise at once:

1. If *aion* means an endless period, how can it have a plural?
2. How did such phrases come to be repeatedly occurring in Scripture where *aion* is added to *aion,* if *aion* is of itself infinite?
3. Why does the Scripture speak of the *aion* or *aions* and

beyond? How can anything be beyond eternity?
4. Why do we repeatedly read of the end of the *aion?*
5. Finally, if *aion* is infinite, why is it applied over and over to things that are finite?

If an *aion* is not infinite, what right do translators have to translate the adjective *aionios,* which depends on *aion* for its meaning, by the terms "eternal" or "everlasting"?

To limit all of God's dealings with people to the narrow span of our earthly existence is to close our eyes to the truer and higher teaching of the Gospel. What does God mean by the many references to "ages" when He speaks in the New Testament of His redeeming plan? Many translators, commentators, and preachers pay no attention to these ages at all. Most translations have so obscured this teaching that it is impossible to see it. Before I started studying this, I had no idea that the same words translated "eternal," "everlasting," "forever," etc., were translated "age" or "ages" in many passages of the New Testament. Is this fair or reasonable? I don't think so, especially when by understanding what they clearly teach we are able to harmonize the terrible threats in God's Word with His clearly expressed purpose to save all mankind.

In these "ages" is revealed the true scope of redemption as a vast plan, extending over many ages, of which our present life is just a very brief part. Through these ages, Christ's redeeming work goes on. Hebrews 13:8 tells us, "Jesus Christ is the same yesterday and today and through the ages." God's purpose and plan for the ages is, according to Ephesians 1:9–10, to unite "ALL things in him [Christ], things in heaven and things on earth." Then, as 1 Corinthians 15:22–28 tells us,

> In Christ shall ALL be made alive. But each in his own order: Christ the firstfruits, then at his coming those who belong to Christ. Then comes the end, when he delivers the kingdom to God the Father after destroying every rule and every authority and power. For he must reign until he has put all his enemies under his feet. The last enemy to be destroyed is

death. [How can there be eternal death if death is destroyed?] For "God has put ALL things in subjection under his feet." But when it says, "all things are put in subjection," it is plain that he is excepted who put all things in subjection under him. When all things are subjected to him, then the Son himself will also be subjected to him who put all things in subjection under him, that God may be all in all.

CHAPTER 13

Objections Answered

*Unfailing love and truth have met together.
Righteousness and peace have kissed!
(Psalm 85:10 NLT)*

What about Matthew 3:12 and Luke 3:17, which say that Christ will burn the chaff with unquenchable fire? This is obviously a hyperbole, which the *World Book Dictionary* defines as "An exaggerated statement used for effect and not meant to be taken literally." As noted earlier, even many of the proponents of everlasting hell no longer believe in literal hellfire. Thomas Allin writes, "Any good lexicon will show us how little the term translated 'unquenchable' really conveys that idea. Homer often applies it to 'glory,' 'laughter,' 'shouting,' to the brief fire that consumed the Grecian fleet. Eusebius twice says that martyrs were consumed in 'unquenchable' fire. Church History 6, 41. Cyril calls the fire, that consumed the burnt offering, unquenchable."

It is terrible to think of the agony caused to loving hearts with regard to their dead loved ones. How can people have any peace or joy if they believe that their loved ones are suffering unspeakable agony in literally unquenchable flames? I urge my readers to pause and seriously consider that to press words like "unquenchable" to a narrow literal meaning is absolute nonsense. Look at Jeremiah 17:4 where God says to Judah, "For in my anger a fire is kindled that shall burn forever." Yet in Romans 11:26, God promises through Paul that "all Israel will be saved." In Jeremiah 30:12, God says to Israel and Judah, "For thus says the Lord: your hurt is incurable." Doesn't incurable mean incurable? Yet, in verse 17, God says, "I will restore health to you, and your wounds I will heal, declares the Lord."

Matthew 10:28: "And do not fear those who kill the body but cannot kill the soul. Rather fear him who can destroy both soul and body in *Gehenna*." This is a favorite passage of annihilationists. They see this verse as teaching that God will annihilate people completely in hell. This is patently absurd. Satan, not God, presides over hell, and he is only able to kill the body. This verse is not about the fate of the wicked but the power of God. If God wanted to, He could annihilate everything, but He doesn't. If this verse were really about the fate of the wicked, it would probably say, "Fear him who is going to destroy both soul and body in hell." But it doesn't say He is going to—only that He can.

Matthew 25:46: "And these [the goats] will go away into eternal punishment, but the righteous into eternal life." It has been pointed out earlier that the word translated "eternal" should be translated "age," which is an indefinite length of time. And the word translated "punishment" should be translated "correction." The verse would then read, "And these will go away into an age of correction, but the righteous into an age of life." The goats go away to be prepared for eventual salvation. Even the word translated "goats" is the word for young goats, implying affection on the part of the Great Shepherd. In Exodus 12:5, in reference to the Passover, it says, "Your lamb shall be without blemish, a male a year old. You may take it from the sheep or from the goats." In the Catacombs, the Good Shepherd is sometimes depicted carrying a baby goat on His shoulders. Surely this is an indication that the early church did not consider the separation of the sheep and the goats to be permanent.

Matthew 12:32: "Whoever speaks against the Holy Spirit will not be forgiven, either in this age or in the age to come." When seeking to interpret a statement made centuries ago in a different language than our own, it makes sense to see how those who spoke that language interpreted it. The understanding that most of the early church fathers had about the sin against the Holy Spirit was not that it was absolutely unpardonable, but that those who were guilty of it would be punished for it both in this age and in the age to come unless they truly repented of it.

Athanasius says of this sin, "If they may obtain pardon, for there is no sin unpardonable with God to them who truly repent." Chrysostom said, "We know that this sin was forgiven to some that repented of it." What is then the meaning of it? That it is a very serious sin, that is harder to be forgiven of than others. That was how Ambrose and other fathers understood it. I believe this is another example of hyperbole, which is, as we noted earlier, defined in *The World Book Dictionary* as "an exaggerated statement used for effect and not meant to be taken literally." Jesus was in effect saying, "Be careful! You are in danger of committing a very serious sin!" Remember that the sin in question according to Matthew 12:32 is speaking against the Holy Spirit. I have personally read the testimonies of people who had done just that and later repented and found forgiveness. I have heard preachers say that this sin is attributing the work of the Holy Spirit to the devil and other such things, but Matthew doesn't say that. It just says it is speaking against the Holy Spirit, a sin that has been committed by many, a very serious sin, but not unforgivable if one truly repents.

What about Hebrews 12:15–17, where the reader is exhorted not to be like Esau, who, "when he desired to inherit the blessing, he was rejected, for he found no chance to repent, though he sought it with tears." This story has nothing to do with salvation. The blessing he failed to receive was the blessing of the firstborn son. But even though Esau lost that blessing and couldn't get it back, Hebrews 11:20 tells us, "By faith Isaac invoked future blessings on Jacob and Esau."

2 Thessalonians 1:9: "They will suffer the punishment of *aionion* destruction, away from the presence of the Lord and from the glory of his might." We have already shown that the word *aionion* means an indefinite period and not eternal, and the word translated "destruction" is the Greek word *olethros,* which is used in 1 Corinthians 5:5 for the destruction of the flesh or the sinful nature, "so that his spirit may be saved in the day of the Lord."

Some argue from 2 Corinthians 6:2, "Behold, now is the day of salvation," that salvation is confined to this life only. But with God, the time is always now. There is no warrant from this passage to limit salvation to this life.

Next we look at Revelation. As we do, let the reader keep in mind that this is a highly figurative book full of strange visions and metaphors. To try to build a case for eternal hell from such a book is absurd. With that in mind, let us look at Revelation 14:9–11: "And another angel, a third, followed them, saying with a loud voice, 'If anyone worships the beast and its image and receives a mark on his forehead or on his hand, he also will drink the wine of God's wrath, poured full strength into the cup of his anger, and he will be tormented with fire and sulfur in the presence of the holy angels and in the presence of the Lamb. And the smoke of their torment goes up for ages and ages, and they have no rest.'"

Being what is called a Partial Preterist, which describes a certain school of eschatology that seems to be held to by R.C. Sproul and Hank Hanegraaff (the Bible Answer Man), among others, I believe this passage is not about the end times, but about the time of the evil emperor Nero, who was believed by many of the early Christians who lived during his brutal reign to be the beast. The sufferings spoken of in this passage would then be speaking of the terrible earthly sufferings that befell Rome at that time. But whatever theory of eschatology one holds to, the passage teaches suffering that is for ages and ages (however long that may be) and not for eternity. Similar language is used in Isaiah 34:9–10, which is clearly not talking about the afterlife but the present (at that time) life: "And the streams of Edom shall be turned into pitch, and her soil into sulfur; her land shall become burning pitch [brimstone]. Night and day it shall not be quenched; its smoke shall go up forever."

I would remind the reader again that the whole Bible is written from an Eastern mindset and is full of metaphors and hyperbole. If such language is taken literally, the meaning is lost. When Scripture writers want to describe the dusky redness of a lunar eclipse, they say the moon has "turned to blood." So it is with the words of Christ. Am I to hate my father and mother? Am I to cut off my limbs or pluck out my eye? Of course not. Neither should we believe that sinners are going to be thrown into the valley of Hinnom and burn forever!

Revelation 21:8: "But as for the cowardly, the faithless, the detestable, as for murderers, the sexually immoral, sorcerers, and all liars, their portion will be in the lake of fire and sulfur, which is the second death." Revelation 20:14 says, "Death and Hades were thrown into the lake of fire." A lake of fire would destroy everything thrown into it. When Death and Hades are thrown into this lake, they will be destroyed. When sinners, who are immortal, are thrown into it, their sins will be destroyed, but they themselves will be saved. See 1 Corinthians 3:12–15 and 5:5.

We are told in Revelation 21:4: "He will wipe away every tear from their eyes, and death shall be no more, neither shall there be mourning nor crying nor pain anymore, for the former things have passed away." This sounds like 2 Peter 3:13: "But according to his promise we are waiting for new heavens and a new earth in which righteousness dwells." This is the glorious future that awaits us: a universe that has been entirely cleansed of sin, where everyone and everything has been restored and reconciled to God, not a universe where many of our friends and relatives are suffering unspeakable torment forever!

I could examine a lot more Scriptures, but I feel I have given the best evidence for the temporary, remedial nature of punishment and the eventual salvation of all of God's children, of whom Christians are but the firstfruits. I have sought to answer the chief objections to this position in a fair and thorough manner. If there are still lingering doubts, I would remind the wavering that to ask for mathematical certainty on these points is to ask for the impossible. No reasonable person expects mathematical proof of the existence of God. No great theological question exists that is not open to some questions, more or less plausible, on scriptural grounds. To ask for irrefutable proof of the larger hope is to ask for what no reasonable person asks for when it comes to similar cases.

The burden of proof falls on those who assert eternal torment for several reasons:

1. Everyone admits that God is a God of love, and nobody

admits that God is cruel.
2. This view is in harmony with the declared will of God to save all men.
3. Because the teaching of eternal hell is unworthy of an Almighty God.
4. Because the popular view is not only cruel, but is also dualistic, while the opposing view rests on the great principle that good is always stronger than evil.
5. Because a promise is more binding than a threat. Take Nineveh, for example. Jonah had no right to be upset when God's threat to destroy Nineveh didn't come to pass. But we have every right to expect Jesus to draw all men to Himself as He has promised to do.

CHAPTER 14

What About Evangelism?

Go into all the world and proclaim the gospel to the whole creation. (Mark 16:15)

If everyone is going to be saved eventually, why evangelize? There are plenty of good reasons for sharing the Good News in God's Word.

The first reason is that God rejoices when people come into a personal relationship with Him through Jesus Christ. No matter what our view is of the afterlife, this should be our primary motivation not only for witnessing but also for everything we do. Colossians 3:23: "Whatever you do, work heartily, as for the Lord and not for men." Colossians 3:17: "And whatever you do, in word or deed, do everything in the name of the Lord Jesus, giving thanks to God the Father through him." 1 Corinthians 10:31: "Whether you eat or drink, or whatever you do, do all to the glory of God." In Luke 15:7, Jesus tells us, "There will be more joy in heaven over one sinner who repents than over ninety-nine righteous persons who need no repentance."

In the parable of the prodigal son, which I like to call the parable of the father who never gives up on his children, the father, who represents God, says to the his older son, "It was fitting to celebrate and be glad, for this your brother was dead, and is alive; he was lost, and is found" (Luke 15:32). If I had a brother who was estranged from our earthly father, my primary motive for wanting to see that brother reconciled to our father would not be the consequences to my brother (like disinheritance), especially assuming the rift was his fault. My primary motive would be to please my father because he is a good and loving father who loves all of his children and wants and deserves their love in return. If you want to bring joy and gladness to your Heavenly Father, tell others about Him!

The next reason we should witness is because God commands it. Matthew 28:18–20: "And Jesus came and said to them [the disciples], 'All authority in heaven and on earth has been given to me. Go therefore and make disciples of all nations, baptizing them in the name of the Father and of the Son and of the Holy Spirit, teaching them to observe all that I have commanded you. And behold, I am with you always, to the end of the age.'" Acts 1:8: "But you will receive power when the Holy Spirit has come upon you, and you will be my witnesses in Jerusalem and in all Judea and Samaria, and to the end of the earth." In Mark 16:15, Jesus said to the eleven, "Go into all the world and proclaim the gospel to the whole creation." If Jesus commands us to tell others the Good News of salvation, we shouldn't need the fear of eternal torment to make us obey Him!

The next reason we should tell others about Jesus is so they can experience the abundant life of following Him now. Jesus said in John 10:10, "I came that they [his sheep] may have life and have it abundantly." The NLT translates this verse: "My purpose is to give life in all its fullness." In John 14:27, Jesus told His disciples, "Peace I leave with you; my peace I give to you." John 14:16–18: "I will ask the Father, and he will give you another Helper, to be with you forever, even the Spirit of truth, whom the world cannot receive, because it neither sees him nor knows him. You know him, for he dwells with you and will be in you. I will not leave you as orphans; I will come to you." John 15:11: "These things I [Jesus] have spoken to you, that my joy may be in you, and that your joy may be full." Philippians 4:11: "I [Paul] have learned in whatever situation I am to be content." Philippians 4:19: "And my God will supply every need of yours according to his riches in glory in Christ Jesus." Do you want your friends and loved ones to have an abundant life filled with the Holy Spirit and peace and joy and contentment? Do you want them to have all their needs met? Tell them about Jesus!

Another reason for telling others about Jesus is when God uses you to draw them closer to Himself, you will have joy! In Luke 10, Jesus sent out seventy or seventy-two disciples on an evangelistic trip, depending on which version you read. Verse 17 says, "The seventy-two returned with joy, saying, 'Lord, even the demons are subject to us in your name!'" Paul said in Philippians 1:18, "Christ is proclaimed, and in that I rejoice!" Paul's letter to the Philippians was written while he was imprisoned for the gospel. The tone of that letter is more joyful than any of his other letters. He repeatedly rejoices about the gospel being preached and people coming to know Jesus. We should be concerned not only with people's destinies but also with the fact that God loves them and wants to have a relationship with them now.

Finally, if people die in their sins, they will be punished! I believe it will not be everlasting, but it will be terrible! And if we love people, we should want to spare them from any suffering.

Summary and Conclusion

The question of Universalism is usually argued as if the main point is man's endless suffering. As odious and repulsive as the idea of endless suffering is, it is not the main point. The vital question is who will win the battle for men's souls, God or the devil? Which is more powerful, righteousness or sin?

The popular creed makes sin eternal, although God's Word says that Jesus came to put away sin. It makes God's wrath eternal, although Scripture says that it is only for a moment. It denies the Scripture in 2 Peter 3:13, which says that we are waiting for a new heaven and a new earth in which righteousness (and by implication, only righteousness) dwells. It never explains how the saints can enjoy heaven while their mothers and fathers, sons and daughters, and husbands and wives are suffering unspeakable agony in hell. It never explains how God can be all in all when there exists a place for all eternity where men and women will join their shrieks of agony with curses and blasphemy toward the God, who claimed to be their Father, but has abandoned them.

What would we think of a woman or a man who took pride in keeping an immaculate house who swept all of the dirt into a room away from the rest of the house? Not only that, but what if she or he cleansed the things in the house that least needed cleaning and reserved only the filthiest things for sweeping into the room? That is what the God of eternal hell does. He cleanses some of the filth in

His house, but the worst of it He sweeps into a "room" called hell, where it's out of sight, out of mind. And worst of all, the dirt He sweeps into this dreadful "room" called hell is not inanimate objects but people—people who for all their faults still have feelings, who have other people who are dear to them and people they are dear to. Worst of all, God, their Creator, once said that He loved them so much that He sent His Son to die for them. Some of them didn't even know about Him and His professed love for them! But now it's too late. They are lost forever!

I have spoken very plainly, because I don't believe that those who teach the traditional view really realize all of the implications of their view. I have spoken very plainly because of the moral scandal involved in lowering God below the level of humanity, because such teaching justly makes God odious to millions. The philosopher Bertrand Russell, who wrote the book *Why I Am Not a Christian*, gave as one of his reasons—that Jesus Christ, the founder of Christianity, believed in and taught eternal hell. This may or may not have been an excuse, but I wish Russell had known that Jesus never taught any such thing!

As earnestly as I can, let me repeat that the choice is between accepting the victory of Christ or of evil. There is no escape from this dilemma. It doesn't change anything to try to minimize the number of the lost or to teach their annihilation. All such modifications leave untouched the main problem with the popular creed, which is the triumph of evil. The eternal existence of sin and rebellion against God is sin triumphant. Sin, which God was unable to remove without annihilating the sinner, is sin triumphant and death victorious.

How strange, too, is the delusion, often advocated today, that all the real objections to the traditional creed are met if the grosser forms of teaching it are abandoned. "We'll still teach eternal punishment, but we won't talk about a literal fire. We'll teach that the torment is spiritual, not physical. We'll rack the spirit with endless regret. We'll hand over to the devil men and women created in God's image, for whom Christ died. It's only forever and ever!" As long as one soul for whom Christ died remains in the devil's grip for ever, to that extent is the devil victorious.

Another vital point is whether or not it is right to describe, as some do, our time here on earth as probation. Is it right to see God primarily as a judge instead of a loving Father? I don't think so. A father has to exercise judgment in raising His children, but that is not how God is portrayed. The God, who is love, is seen as a stern judge with gavel raised, eager to pronounce sentence. Instead of the mercy seat, the seat of judgment is presented to our eyes. An inflexible code and an unbending judge rule all. Love is subordinate, and sin becomes the central fact. Guilt, not grace, comes first. Such a system may call itself the Gospel and point to the greatest names for support, and it may be taught from thousands of pulpits, but it is not the true Gospel!

Where is the joy in Christianity today? Where is the winsomeness that was evident in our Lord that attracted great crowds who just wanted to be near Him? How can a believer have joy when it appears that evil is triumphing? And it is, if all of these self-absorbed, self-indulgent people we're surrounded by are heading for everlasting separation from God, who loves them and wants to fill their existence with love, joy, and meaning.

I repeat what I said earlier, that Universalists believe in the punishment of the unrepentant. But we believe that it is meant to bring about their repentance. To punish forever is neither loving nor just, but is pure sadism. We do not teach that God is an indulgent grandfather who winks at sin, but only that His punishment is both in proportion to sins committed and is remedial. It is those who teach everlasting punishment who make light of sin by saying that God is unable to eradicate it. Every form of partial salvation is rooted in selfishness. This selfishness is largely unconscious, but all too real.

I am shocked at the unwillingness of Christians to even examine the claims of Universalism! I believe that for many, the idea is in the back of their mind: "If there is no eternal hell, maybe there is no eternal heaven." I don't know of anything more shocking than the thought of the saints being filled with bliss in heaven while their loved ones suffer in hell! The heaven of the traditional creed is a thing so hardened, so awful, that just to think about it fills the mind with horror. How the saints can be happy in heaven while their loved ones suffer in eternal hell is a mystery. It is hell disguised as heaven! "Maybe," some will answer, "God will wipe away the memory of lost love ones." Would you want that? The movie *The Forgotten* is about aliens who abduct a plane full of children and try to erase all trace of their existence. One mother, even before she realizes her son is still alive, recoils at the thought of ever forgetting him. As a father, her response resonated with me. If I lost one of my children, I would not want to forget them, even if it would ease the pain of losing them.

One of the worst things about the traditional creed is that it teaches us to forgive our enemies while at the same time God refuses to forgive His. It teaches that God, who hates sin and sent Jesus to take it away, has prepared a place for its eternal existence. It teaches that be cause sin is so hateful to God, it must go on forever in hell. The blessed are content to gaze peacefully on the abyss of hell, their satisfaction unbroken, their joys undimmed if not actually increased by the torments of the lost, and this they call the triumph of the cross?

Dante, in his book *The Inferno,* has a sign posted over the gates of hell that reads, "Abandon hope, ye who enter here." If the traditional teaching about everlasting hell is true, there should be a sign over the gates of heaven: "Abandon love and sympathy, ye who enter here."

There is a an old hymn that goes in part: "O saints of God, forever blest, in that dear home how sweet your rest." How sweet your rest, O wives whose husbands forever burn! O mothers, how sweet your rest while your children live on and on in agony forever! In that dear home, how sweet your rest!

Some people who don't even want to think about the implications of the traditional creed content themselves by saying, "Whatever happens, I know God will do what is best for everyone." But how can this be true if the traditional creed is true? What are the facts according to that creed? That Almighty God, who was perfectly free to create people or not, created myriad hapless people knowing that their eternal destiny was to suffer unspeakable agony forever! How can that be best for anyone?

It is amazing to me how few are willing to even fairly examine this position. But it is even more amazing how few will follow it to its logical conclusion, which is to joyfully embrace it and cast off the false Romish doctrine of eternal torment!

It is pure sophistry to say as someone said to me, "You can't bring human reasoning into it. You have to go by what the Bible says." As though that wasn't the very thing I was seeking to do! If the Bible didn't make sense, I wouldn't believe it. But it does when you use sanctified reason instead of just accepting everything on the surface. Why should I give up my ideas of mercy, justice, and love when it is God who gave them to me through His Word and His Spirit? If our human ideas of right and wrong can't be trusted when applied to God, anything could happen! Anything may be right; anything may be wrong! Anything may be true; anything may be false! All is chaos and anarchy. Heaven and hell may change places, and so, for all we know, may good and evil! That the heart is deceitful and desperately wicked was not written about the regenerate heart!

I have shown that Christian Universalism is a view that was widely held in the early church before it became corrupted with paganism in the fourth century. I have shown that the words translated "eternal" and "everlasting" are mistranslations and should be uniformly translated "age," as they are in many places in modern translations. As to the charge that Universalism leads to moral laxity, I don't think anyone would charge William Law with laxity after reading *A Serious Call to a Devout and Holy Life*. He was a Christian Universalist. I don't think you could justly call Hannah Whitehall Smith morally lax . Her book *The Christian's Secret of a Happy Life* is a classic on the deeper Christian life, the life of holiness and entire devotion to Christ. She too believed in the wider hope. Frederick Faber, whom A.W. Tozer quoted so much, believed in it too. His classic hymn, "There's a Wideness in God's Mercy," used to be found in many hymnals. Athanasius, the great champion of the Trinity, believed it too. These were all orthodox Christians, not liberals or heretics.

I have earnestly sought to be fair and accurate in everything I have said. Here I would make a final appeal to my readers to try to think about these things with an open mind and heart and recognize them for what they are—the only views worthy of an Almighty, just, and loving God. This hope alone explains the wonders of our creation in God's image. It alone shows the true majesty of love and its unquenchable thirst to save finally the most hopeless sinners. It alone teaches that with God, "all things are possible." It alone sweetens every sorrow and wipes away every tear.

Hope is what I offer to those who have lost loved ones to death, not knowing where they stood with God. Or for those who have loved ones who are still alive but are not walking with God. God loves them. Christ died for them. He has promised to draw all men to Himself! He is not finished with them yet! He will seek them until He finds them and carries them safely home at last! Don't lose hope! The End.

Anyone who would like to contact me can call me at 805-258-3318 or write me at this address:

Mark T. Chamberlain
601 Galerita St.
Oxnard, CA 93030

Bibliography

C.S. Lewis. *Mere Christianity.* Macmillan Publishing Co., Inc., 1943, 1945, 1952.

C.S. Lewis. *Surprised by Joy.* Collins, Fontana Books, 1981.

Jonathan Hill. *The History of Christian Thought.* InterVarsity Press, 2003.

Printed in the United States
103732LV00002B/279/A